THE TOTAL VEGETARIAN
COOKBOOK

sweet · savory · simple

THE TOTAL VEGETARIAN
COOKBOOK

sweet • savory • simple

More than **150** Outstanding Vegan Recipes from the *StepFast* Kitchen

BARBARA WATSON

Forewords by Neil Nedley, MD
and Jane Kurtz, RN, RD, MPH

AMAZING FACTS

Roseville, CA

Acknowledgements

My sincere thanks to:

Deanna Willett, an outstanding cook and teacher, who shared with me the basics of vegan cuisine and whose creative talent inspired me to develop recipes of my own;

The countless health guests and seminar participants who not only complimented my cooking, but who implemented lifestyle changes and regained their health, thereby encouraging me to keep cooking and sharing;

The Potomac Conference of Seventh-day Adventists and the Ardmore Institute of Health, parent corporation of the Lifestyle Center of America, who together enabled me to begin sharing this powerful message of healthful living through the *StepFast Lifestyle Series*;

Barbara Hesslegrave and Jean Marie Smith for lending their editorial skills and providing valuable feedback;

My family and friends for tolerating many culinary experiments and giving me honest opinions and helpful suggestions;

The many friends who have shared recipe ideas with me over the years, including Zinia Agosto, Julianne Aranda, the Benton sisters, Melissa Bradshaw, Kae Borrero, Dan and Ellen Butler, Janet Evert, Raquel Garcia, Geraldine Hollis, Kathy Mountjoy, Erica Nedley, Pat Pagan, Robert Pannekoek, Dyane Pergerson, Joann Rachor, Paula Reiter, Ronda Smith, Peggy Spangler, Sebastian Teh, and others;

My daughter Charlotte (Charlie), for sharing her talent in food styling, her exceptional organizational skills, and her positive attitude, all of which made writing this book a fun project and helped tremendously in getting it to press;

Greg Solie at Altamont Graphics, for his excellent work in the design and layout of the book;

Amazing Facts, whose effective and far-reaching ministry addresses the needs of the whole person, for making the publishing of this book possible; René Paille, my wonderful husband, for his love and encouragement and for the beautiful images of the recipes;

Most important, my heavenly Father, for all that He has taught me about His marvelous plan for health, happiness, and the eternal abundant life, and for giving me so many wonderful opportunities to share these principles with others.

Published by Amazing Facts, Inc.
P. O. Box 1058
Roseville, CA 95678-8058
800-538-7275
www.AmazingFacts.org

Cover Design by Haley Trimmer
Principal Photography by René Paille
Layout by Greg Solie • AltamontGraphics.com

ISBN 978-1-5801938-0-1

Table of Contents

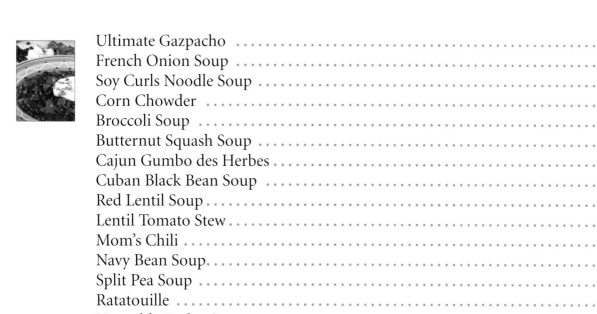

Dedication

In memory of my mother, Christine M. Watson, affectionately called "Teenie" because of her small stature and her wonderful ability to make people smile.

On her 80th birthday, we presented my mother with Joan Collins' book of secrets to health, youth, and happiness, not because she needed them, but because she had already written the book on how to stay young and beautiful. We thought she might like to compare notes with another picture of success.

Looking young and beautiful were not the only goals of Teenie's healthy lifestyle program. A wife and the mother of five children, she had a sales career and did lots of volunteer work. She also loved to entertain, so she needed plenty of energy. Health information was not as readily available when my mother started searching in the 60s as it is today. She did learn to eat lean and found a recipe for "Tiger's Milk," guaranteed to make you grab the world by the tail. A combination of brewer's yeast, reconstituted powdered milk, and blackstrap molasses, it was quite a dose! But she drank it faithfully, and at the time, I really appreciated that she didn't make her children drink it!

When I became a vegetarian, Mama was in her mid-70s and was eager to receive all the health information I had to share. Soymilk and ground flax seed soon became a part of her morning meal. Blueberries also became a steady part of her diet when she read about a "new thrill on Blueberry Hill!" A cancer survivor following a mastectomy at age 52, she was anxious to include any high-antioxidant foods in her diet. After learning that blueberries are chock-full of antioxidants, she made them standard fare on her breakfast menu.

I have my mother to thank for teaching me the basics of cooking. At a young age, it was one of my favorite pastimes, and she never made me feel that I was in the way. In fact, she was very happy for me to take over the kitchen whenever I wanted!

Christine M. "Teenie" Watson

Though she taught me lots about how to cook, Mama taught me more about how to live. Her bookshelves housed her Bible and titles on two subjects: health and the Christian life. Her spiritual health flourished, and she also came to understand the relationship between nutrition and health. She accepted her responsibility to take care of her mind and body while on earth, all the while clinging to the promises of the Savior, looking forward to eternal life with Him.

Trusting that He always knows best, we often heard her recite Romans 8:28, "We know that all things work together for good to those who love God," going forward in faith even when life dealt a difficult blow. She looked to the Lord for strength and often quoted Philippians 4:13, "I can do all things through Christ who strengthens me." When faced with situations that prompted doubt, she always said, "I just live by faith and trust," and she did.

Mama lived to see her 89th birthday and still looked beautiful, with hardly a wrinkle in her face. Though she had a propensity to worry, she chose to cast her cares upon God. We found in her journal this prayer:

"Give us a new assurance of Thy love, and a new sense of the dignity and value of life. We pray Thee that we may be able to say when our call comes, 'Glad did I live and glad do I die, and I lay me down with a will.'"

God answered that prayer because she loved life, lived responsibly, and followed her own advice:

"Always look on the bright side!"

Foreword
by Neil Nedley, MD

Our Creator designed us to thrive and experience health, vitality, and joy without the looming threat of disease and premature death. Unfortunately, the violation of health-promoting principles and practices has robbed countless individuals of the happy, long, and productive life they might otherwise have opportunity to enjoy.

The health and lifestyle connection is now embraced by many on a personal level, by organizations on a corporate level, and acknowledged by healthcare czars throughout the nation. Recommendations for diet, exercise, and stress management aimed at addressing weight loss, heart disease, and cancer permeate all media. From community health fairs to scientific studies to news services, the message is consistent: Diet and lifestyle have a profound impact on the health we experience.

In my Internal Medicine practice, few things are as rewarding as witnessing a patient take hold of the concept that disease can be prevented and even reversed by incorporating a healthy lifestyle and, specifically, a vegetarian diet. Yet all who come to acknowledge the relationship between what we do and what we experience need practical help in implementing the choices they desire to make.

Fortunately, teaching tools are now available to make adopting an optimum lifestyle not only possible, but also help us to overcome its challenges with progressive energy and enjoyment.

Barbara Watson is the creator of one such tool, the *StepFast Lifestyle Series*, a dynamic lifestyle education video program. In the book you have in your hands, Barbara provides not only simple, delicious recipes from the *StepFast* series, but also additional, newly developed recipes and menus that give a wonderful nutritional boost to your diet. *The Total Vegetarian Cookbook* is a tremendous help to those looking for a convenient way to enjoy the taste and enjoyment of eating a total vegetarian diet.

Neil Nedley, MD
Author of *Proof Positive,*
How to Reliably Combat Disease
and Achieve Optimal Health
through Nutrition and Lifestyle
www.nedleypublishing.com

Foreword
by Jane Kurtz, RN, RD, MPH

From a single cell the miracle begins. Dividing and multiplying again and again, it soon forms the 75 trillion cells making up the human body. Concealed in the nucleus of each one is a DNA blueprint that determines the unique function of that particular cell. Brain, muscle, bone, skin, lung, and liver cells—over 200 types working together to create you! What a miracle. What a gift!

As a newborn, you had brand-new cells. When they became damaged and aged, they were replaced by one of the billions of fresh replacement cells formed daily. The process still continues. Your body is a phenomenal building project. The work crews never quit!

Red blood cells live and do their job for about four months, then they are dismantled and new red blood cells take their place. White blood cells are replaced daily, while stomach lining cells are replaced every two days and colon cells every four days. Every three to four weeks, you get a whole new skin and even your bones are in a continual recycling process. Approximately every 25 years you have a new skeleton!

Just as a carpenter needs precision tools and quality building materials to produce a solid structure, your body needs a steady supply of proper nutrients to build healthy tissue. Making billions of new cells every day is an enormous task for your internal construction crew. If you provide quality building materials and the right tools to do the job, your newly formed cells will be strong and healthy just like your original cells. Supplies for this remarkable project are chosen and delivered to the construction site several times each day by the food that goes into your mouth.

Packed into natural foods are the very best building materials, "macronutrients," that God has created—nourishing carbohydrates, wholesome proteins, and beneficial fats. Rich in fiber, essential vitamins, minerals, and phytonutrients, natural foods also contain the tools or "micronutrients" needed to produce strong, healthy cells. Although our builders are amazingly adaptable, they depend on the building supplies we choose. We have the option of providing top-quality resources or inferior, damaged, or depleted materials.

For example, providing lots of hydrogenated and saturated fats to the construction site results in cell membranes that are stiff and rigid, contributing to disease. When we choose unsaturated fats, those same cell membranes become fluid and flexible—a healthy, normal condition.

Refined and processed foods have been stripped of most of their valuable "micronutrients." Consuming too much white flour, white rice, and white sugar, which make up the majority of pre-packaged convenience foods, causes us to be overfed and undernourished. Hampered by poor quality, it's as if our internal construction crews have to use Styrofoam for bricks, masking tape instead of nails, and plastic knives in place of power saws.

Sooner or later the project falls apart. Immune systems that should ward off disease begin to let germs in and take over. Arteries that are normally flexible become hardened and clogged. Bones crumble with osteoporosis. We age faster. We wear out sooner.

But who would construct a building with masking tape instead of nails? Who would use tissue paper instead of solid timbers? You might be surprised! It has a lot to do with what we have for dinner, along with the rest of our lifestyle habits. While our choices each day over a lifetime can CONTRIBUTE to disease, the good news is that our choices day by day over a lifetime can also help PREVENT illness.

Bursting with vital nutrients, the recipes contained in *The Total Vegetarian Cookbook* are carefully designed using a wide variety of natural foods. These are the high-quality tools and building materials your body's construction crews crave! Have fun as you discover how delicious wholesome eating can be—and in the long run, enjoy the sparkle of "well constructed" vitality. May you prosper and be in health,

Jane Kurtz, MPH, RD, RN

Why Total Vegetarian?

*I*t's been said that vegetarians not only eat a plant-based diet, they're convinced that everybody else should too! I confess that I am, unashamedly, one of those people. And why wouldn't I share the incredible advantages of adopting a total vegetarian diet? It not only helps the individual, it also benefits the animals and the planet!

In fact, someone just recently asked me to explain why I am a vegetarian. "Is it to protect the environment … for health reasons … for spiritual reasons?" I was delighted to answer, "It is all of these." And if I had the time to say more, I would have also added two more reasons: ethical concerns and the pocketbook. For those who want to probe more deeply into these reasons, allow me to elaborate a little.

All five reasons are valid and important, but none affects us so directly as the personal health benefits, so that's where I'll begin.

Health Benefits

The message has never been more clear: Consuming meat and other animal products plays a direct role in the demise of our health through the onset of degenerative diseases, including the number one killer in America — heart disease. But the overwhelming good news is that the risks of developing this disease and others, such as diabetes, kidney disease, cancer, and a host of others including obesity, which is now considered a medical disease, are potentially avoidable when we choose a plant-based diet.

A total vegetarian — or vegan — diet, contrary to popular belief, can be very flavorful, and it usually includes a much wider variety of foods than those consumed by the average meat eater. Plus by adopting a vegetarian diet, not only do we avoid the risks presented by consuming animal products, we benefit from colorful fruits and vegetables; whole grains; nuts and legumes, all of which provide an abundance of vitamins, minerals, and antioxidant packages that go to work to help protect our cells against heart disease and invading cancers.

Additionally, plant foods contain more of the nutrients needed to ward off depression and anxiety disorders, a growing problem in our fast-paced society.

So the ideal diet means ideal weight, increased energy, disease prevention, and a brighter outlook. In my opinion and in the opinion of science, nothing could make more sense than to enjoy these benefits while delving into delicious vegetarian cuisine.

Environmental Conservation

Producing food from animals is costly and places a drain on our natural resources, taking approximately 50 times as much fossil fuel and 3 to 15 times as much water to produce as compared to plant protein. Our agricultural process takes up to 16 pounds of grain and soybeans to produce one pound of beef and about five pounds to produce one pound of turkey or eggs. Bypassing the animal and eating plant foods directly translates into a significant conservation of resources.

Even small changes in meat consumption can make a significant global impact on grain stores and food available to feed the poor. Cited in Dr. Neil Nedley's book *Proof Positive*, on page 473, is a calculation from Worldwatch, one of the most respected environmental organizations: Worldwide annual consumption of grain by livestock is 630 million tons. By reducing meat eating by 10 percent, a corresponding 10 percent reduction of grain consumption would occur, conserving 63 million tons of grain, which could be used to feed the growth in the world population for more than two years.

Unfortunately, as nations become more affluent, meat eating increases and steps up the demand for its production. Ironically, they are soon faced with the same health and environmental issues we deal with in our culture. However, if education and awareness accompany this rise in the standard of living, consumers can choose to live responsibly, protecting their health and conserving valuable resources.

As you can see, even with this brief look at dietary choices and the environment, the best diet for individual health is also the optimal diet in terms of conservation, compassion for others, and social consciousness.

Ethical Concerns

Okay. Here's a shocking "in your face" figure you might never have considered: The average meat eater is responsible for the deaths of some 2,400 animals during his or her lifetime. Because meat is something ordered in a restaurant or picked up at the grocery store, no one really thinks about the carnage that occurs in order to make this provision.

And if the deaths of these animals is not sobering enough, we must also understand that the existence of most livestock in factory farms is so miserable that death is a blessing. The conditions often produce hotbeds of disease that endanger the lives of the animals. That might seem like a moot point, but the diseases might also be passed on to the consumer. I love to relax when serving guests, resting assured that by using no animal products, a meal at my table will not include viruses, antibiotics, or prions.

The Pocketbook

One objection often raised about a vegetarian diet is that it is expensive. It is true that commercially prepared vegan foods might be somewhat more expensive than meat, eggs, and dairy products. Pricey meat substitutes, non-dairy cheeses, confections, and ice cream are available, but most of these items are unnecessary. In many cases these products are highly refined and high in fat, sugar, and sodium, and most of them lack the quality and flavor of home-cooked recipes.

This is not to say that some commercial vegetarian products could not be used in moderation. Some contain high-quality ingredients and make meal preparation more convenient. One of my favorites is SoyCurls, a very economical meat substitute. Made from whole soybeans, these little morsels have a texture similar to chicken and can be used in scores of recipes.

Sometimes, a commercial product might contain all plant-based ingredients but offers few health benefits. For an example, a non-dairy ice cream made from soy or rice is a welcomed treat from time to time. However, one-half cup of many brands contains 15 to 19 grams of sugar, over 10 grams of fat, and costs about 75 cents per serving. For half that price, you could enjoy an entire cup of thick strawberry smoothie with all natural sugar, valuable nutrients, and virtually no fat.

When counting the cost of going vegetarian, be sure to consider that meat, cheese, and eggs will no longer take up a portion of your grocery bill. You will likely find a surplus in your budget after purchasing the simpler ingredients needed for vegetarian recipes. Some specialty items are called for in a few of the recipes in *The Total Vegetarian Cookbook,* but many recipes can be prepared with ingredients from your grocery store.

Let's take a look at the per-pound price of protein sources:

Steak	Roast Beef
$11.49	$4.99
Hamburger	Ground Round
$2.29	$3.99
Veal Cutlets	Pork Chops
$4.99	$4.99
Chicken (boned)	Tofu
$3.99	$2.79
SoyCurls	
$1.50	

Clearly the price of animal protein far exceeds the cost of plant-based protein. The potential expense of healthcare costs for lifestyle-related illnesses is also something else to consider in this equation.

Take a look at the bottom line: A low-fat, antioxidant-rich vegetarian diet allows you to eat more, weigh less, and pay less. Now that makes good financial sense.

Spiritual Considerations

When making food choices, not only should we consider personal and global responsibility, the treatment of animals and our own physical and mental health, our spiritual health should be considered as well, two aspects of which I would like to address.

The first is our call to stewardship. When we realize that we are created beings, designed to reflect the image of God, and are called to be faithful stewards of our minds and bodies, a natural result is to desire to live responsibly. Scripture enjoins us in 1 Corinthians 10:31, "whether you eat or drink, or whatever you do, do all to the glory of God." Once we become enlightened regarding the optimum diet to promote health, conserve resources, and show compassion to animals, we realize it is not Christ-like to serve our flesh with an expensive diet that involves extensive carnage and promotes the premature death of God's creatures.

When considering personal health, what a blessing it is to enjoy the bounties God has provided in the plant kingdom while reducing the need for medication and the risk of lifestyle-related diseases. How awesome it is to witness the miracle of health and healing when we demonstrate good stewardship of our bodies, as well as our planet, and cooperate with God's plan for our lives.

The second consideration I want to discuss is regarding the clarity of thought and mental health that we experience, which influences our availability for communion with our Creator. The health of the brain, the organ through which we communicate with God, is dependent upon what we feed it. While this includes what we see, what we read, as well as what we breathe, our diet plays a significant role in the health of the brain.

The temple of God's Spirit is the human mind; this is where we invite Him to dwell within us. Preparing a dwelling place that is not burdened by mental dullness because of poor lifestyle choices should be a major consideration for us all.

Many realize that a high-fat diet can decrease alertness and mental acuity, and we also know that excessive amounts of sugar can cloud the mind as well. In addition, optimum functioning of the brain is dependent upon the inclusion of particular nutrients including B vitamins, omega-3 essential fatty acid, and tryptophan, to name just a few. The recipes presented in this cookbook are designed with these nutrition facts in mind.

Physical exercise, consuming adequate water, and getting proper rest are also important habits to establish to reach optimum brain function, so that our minds will be a ready dwelling place for the Holy Spirit of God. What a blessing to have a role in preparing a personal habitation for Him!

So there you have it: my philosophy and convictions regarding diet, health, responsibility, and spirituality. Others must be in agreement because vegetarians are cropping up all over! If you are beginning to share this philosophy, but wonder if you really possess the power to live according to it, there's good news. The beauty of God's plan is that He doesn't leave us alone to make difficult lifestyle choices. As we invite God to dwell within us, He makes His power available to us to provide the resolve we need to live by our convictions.

Jesus said, "I have come that ye might have life, and that you might have it more abundantly." Each day it will get easier to take charge of your health as your human efforts are combined with Divine power, while new tastes are developed and healthy habits formed. Ask, and you *shall* receive!

The Total Vegetarian Cookbook Solves Two Common Dilemmas

Upwards of 10 million people have become vegetarians, depending upon whom you ask — and when you ask them! For instance, a woman recently told me that she is a "flexitarian!"

I believe people lose their resolve to adopt a vegetarian diet for several reasons, but two stand out in my mind.

First, people find they lack enjoyable food choices. And second, they do not have the resources to easily learn the techniques to prepare delicious, healthful meals. Of course, no one would argue that we need to enjoy our food!

For the *StepFast Lifestyle Series* and now for *The Total Vegetarian Cookbook,* I have designed and collected recipes that solve these two dilemmas: The recipes are incredibly delicious, are easy to prepare, and can be made with readily available ingredients. These vegan recipes have been developed in response to palates hungering for favorite and familiar food, but without the animal products. They have been tested with vegetarians as well as die-hard meat eaters, and both have responded with a cook's favorite compliment: "May I have more, please?"

You will find that *The Total Vegetarian Cookbook* contains a broad variety of more than 150 superb recipes, with easy and concise preparation instructions and flavors and textures bold enough to suppress anyone's desire to look back. I now invite you to "taste and see" that the Lord wants you to both eat well and live well.

So happy cooking and bon appétit!

Welcome to my kitchen!

It's Time to StepFast

So what is *StepFast*? It's new energy! Newfound freedom! A conservation program! It's a lifestyle education program on DVD that will teach you all you need to know about living a healthy lifestyle.

A conservation program? *StepFast* is a program that conserves time, energy, your money, and the earth's resources. And best of all, as you follow the *StepFast* lifestyle principles, you'll enjoy better health and be more available to "step fast" in pursuit of the endeavors to which you are called.

How do you spell a healthy lifestyle?

S-t-e-p-F-a-s-t!

A concise way to describe the *StepFast* lifestyle is to spell out the acronym that represents the *StepFast* healthy principles:

Sunshine

Temperance

Exercise

Proper Diet

Fabulous Water

Air, Pure & Fresh

Sleep, Recreation, and Rest

Trust in God

Sunshine: The first and easiest step to take, getting some sunshine, has tremendous benefits. Providing vitamin D, which promotes bone mineralization, sunshine also lowers blood cholesterol and blood sugar, boosts the immune system, and helps us fight fatigue and depression.

Temperance: By definition, it is abstaining from that which is harmful and wisely employing that which is good, and this applies to all the *StepFast* principles. But further, it is establishing balance in the personal and spiritual areas of your life, investing time in relationships with family and friends, and reaching out in service to others.

Exercise: Dr. David DeRose and exercise physiologist Harold Mayer, at the Lifestyle Center of America, are the key presenters on exercise in the *StepFast* series. Driven home are the power of exercise and the need to make it practical. Dr. DeRose states, "If you could put it in a pill, exercise would be one of the best-selling medications," because the benefits are so astounding. Mayer gives us lots of information about exercise, and the bottom line is: "The exercise for you is the one you will do!"

Proper Diet: The *StepFast* program makes it clear that a total vegetarian diet need not be boring. Fruits, grains, nuts, and vegetables are prepared in appealing and tasty ways — and provide all the nutrients our bodies need.

Fabulous Water: From decreasing the risk of heart attack, to making our skin look soft and younger, to relieving headaches and helping us fight fatigue, water is an amazing beverage! We can't live long without water, and we enjoy better health with lots of it, at least six to eight glasses a day, or one ounce for every two pounds of body weight.

Air, Pure & Fresh: Breathe deeply of pure, fresh air, and be sure to exercise in the great outdoors so your blood will be well oxygenated. Living in the country away from the hustle and bustle of the city has many benefits, one of which is cleaner, fresher air. Also, be sure the air you breathe is cigarette smoke-free.

Sleep, Recreation, and Rest: Studies have shown that to be at our best, we need eight to nine hours of sleep per night. In addition to sleep, proper rest includes relaxation and true re-creation. Spend time out in nature with family and friends. And remember, God created the Sabbath day for us to rest, to commune with Him, and to enjoy fellowship with one another so that we can get our physical and spiritual batteries recharged.

Trust in God: All power for us to walk in harmony with God's plan for health comes from our Creator. To exercise our will by His grace and engage in an active, healthy lifestyle is an inestimable blessing that He wants us to experience. Getting to know Jesus as our Friend and Savior is the key. Managing stress according to biblical principles, engaging in service to others, and manifesting an attitude of gratitude will make the difference.

These components of good health are the foundational principles of the *StepFast Lifestyle Series*, a dynamic, 12-part video series from which you will learn to enjoy a delicious, total vegetarian diet; engage in a simple, energizing, exercise program; and be empowered and de-stressed by a disciplined spiritual life.

Presentations are given by leading preventive healthcare specialists and include lectures on heart disease, weight control, diabetes, hypertension, cancer, osteoporosis, and more. Demonstrations are given of many of the recipes in *The Total Vegetarian Cookbook,* and a professional exercise physiologist provides exercise instruction. Companion materials are provided in the *StepFast Resource Guide* on CD-ROM, which is designed for facilitating the *StepFast Lifestyle Series*. Visit www.stepfast.org or call 888-682-5805 to learn more.

Meals That Heal

Theories abound about the best way to lose weight, prevent disease, and stay healthy. One fad diet after another appears on the scene, some with a "have your bacon and eat it too" philosophy, but the facts are in: Proof positive evidence says that the best way to stay fit and healthy is the combination of a total vegetarian diet and plenty of exercise. Why does this simple, back-to-basics approach seem so difficult?

I believe it is a combination of two misconceptions about food. Number one, we develop preferences for certain foods and think only these can satisfy our palate, and two, we tend to believe that certain foods are nutritionally essential for health.

Dr. Agatha Thrash, M.D., board specialist in pathology says, "There are no essential foods, only essential nutrients." These nutrients can be obtained from many different foods, and if open-minded and willing to develop a palate that appreciates healthier nutritional sources, we can significantly lower our health risks and, I believe, enjoy our food even more.

When a sense of enhancing one's health and contributing to the world's conservation efforts accompanies the partaking of delicious food, satisfaction is multiplied. The blessing of becoming informed, exercising self-control, and making healthy food choices pays large dividends.

A total vegetarian dietary plan is said to consist of four food groups: fruits, vegetables, grains, and nuts. I like to divide the vegetable category in two, distinguishing legumes from other vegetables since they are higher in protein and are a ready substitute for meat and other animal products, thus creating a fifth food group.

The legume category consists of beans, lentils, and peas; it includes tofu as well. Legumes are high in protein, fiber, and other valuable nutrients, but are simply overlooked by most Americans even though their wonderful flavors are enjoyed by millions in other cultures around the world. *The Total Vegetarian Cookbook* will help to reintroduce this valuable nutrient

"Let thy food be thy medicine and thy medicine be thy food."
—Hippocrates

source through numerous recipes that are absolutely delicious and easy to make.

Lacto-ovo vegetarians, while avoiding all flesh foods, include eggs and dairy products in their diet. While some insist that animal products are essential to good nutrition, too much evidence points to the mounting risks of bacterial contamination, harmful viruses, and antibiotic and hormone use in the production of these products. In addition to these risks, many have discovered they are lactose-intolerant or otherwise sensitive to animal products, avoid these products for these reasons.

It has been well established through numerous clinical trials that greater benefits and fewer health risks are associated with a vegan diet. In fact, with the possible exception of vitamin B-12, all nutrients are much more plentiful in a total vegetarian diet, especially those powerful phytochemicals (plant chemicals). Some individuals can develop B-12 deficiencies because of poor absorption; therefore, a supplement or fortified foods are recommended for all. In countries where supplements or fortified foods are not available, the inclusion of small amounts of eggs and/or dairy products is recommended.

For the purpose of discussion in this book, the term "vegan" refers only to a total vegetarian diet and does not refer to employing or avoiding animal products for other uses, nor does it preclude the use of honey.

12 Tips for a Vibrant Total Vegetarian Diet

1 Vary Your Veggies – Before we knew about vitamins, minerals, and phytochemicals, it was easy to get the proper amounts of these nutrients because God color-coded our food! Choosing dark green ensures us calcium and other nutrients, while red and orange veggies give us beta carotene, lycopene, and other antioxidants. Now we know the importance of colorful vegetables; it turns out there are thousands of phytochemicals in our vegetables that pour the benefits into our food.

And don't forget the onions and garlic! The allium family of vegetables includes onions, garlic, leeks, scallions, and chives, which could be instrumental in addressing elevated blood pressure and high cholesterol, as well as bacteria and yeast infections. What a blessing that most savory dishes get their rudimentary flavor base from onions and garlic. Steam up onions and garlic to serve with an otherwise plain burger and you'll get rave reviews.

2 Discover Fiber-rich Fruit – Choose whole fresh fruit instead of juice to get the full benefit of nature's original fast food. As Dr. Zeno Charles-Marcel, MD internal medicine says, "Choose fruit, the whole fruit, and nothing but the fruit!" And eating edible skins will give you lots of fiber as well as other nutrients. With this in mind, whenever possible, go organic.

To remove pesticide residues, make a fruit and vegetable wash by mixing in a sink or basin:

> 2 tablespoons lemon juice
> 1 tablespoon salt
> 2 gallons water
>
> Allow the produce to soak for
> about a minute, then scrub
> slightly and rinse well.

For optimum digestion, eat fruits at one meal and vegetables at another. Keep in mind that anything that contains seeds is a fruit, botanically speaking. This means that tomatoes, cucumbers, and squashes are actually fruits and combine successfully with other fruits for most people.

3 Go With the Grains – Whole grains, of course. And be adventuresome! Try some quinoa, amaranth, and millet along with barley, kamut, and spelt berries. All of these are simple to prepare in a crockpot and are simply delicious. Brown rice, whole wheat, and oats, as well as stone-ground cornmeal, are always good choices, as they provide essential vitamins and minerals that have been stripped from refined flours and most commercial products.

4 Watch Sodium Intake – What should you be looking for? Though no "recommended daily allowance" for sodium has been established, a salt-restricted diet would allow 400 mg. of sodium, and a moderate use of salt would be about a teaspoon a day, or 2400 mg. Remember that many foods naturally contain sodium. If you are serving a recipe that is fairly high in sodium, be sure to balance it with side dishes that are lower in sodium. Try granulated dulse on vegetables and nutritional yeast flakes with a small amount of olive oil on popcorn, both delicious ways to minimize the need for salt.

5 Make Legumes a Mainstay – Legumes comprise a large food category in which there are thousands of varieties of dried beans, peas, peanuts, and lentils. Most cultures feature a grain and legume combination that is a mainstay for that population. South America's beans, rice, and tortillas; Asia's rice and tofu; India's lentils and chapattis; the Middle East's hummus and pita bread — all parallel America's favorite: the peanut butter and jelly sandwich!

Richer in protein than any other plant food, legumes are low in fat, contain B vitamins, and lots of minerals. The fiber in beans helps to stabilize blood sugar and should be included in each day's menu. Canned beans are convenient, but fresh cooked beans have better flavor and texture. Crockpot cookery again provides a convenient way to prepare this staple from scratch. See page 136 for the recipe.

If you seem to have trouble digesting beans, pouring off and changing the water during soaking or cooking helps to get rid of this problem. Serving beans with fresh pineapple might also be helpful.

Tofu, SoyCurls, beans, peas, and lentils of various colors fall into the nutrient-rich category of legumes. So be sure to incorporate some into your diet every day.

6 Get a Little Nutty – A handful a day of nuts and seeds provide satiety, the right kind of fat, and an essential nutritional boost. Studies show that nuts are helpful in safeguarding the heart. Raw nuts are best, and all nuts and seeds should be stored in the refrigerator or freezer.

7 Max the Flax – Two tablespoons a day of ground flaxseed will help prevent constipation and provide 4 grams of omega-3 essential fatty acid. Omega-3 has been found to be beneficial in the prevention and treatment of depression, to assist with normalizing triglycerides, and in giving the immune system a boost. If flax oil is taken, only 1½ to 2 teaspoons is needed to provide about the same amount of omega-3. Many who use 1 tablespoon of flax oil each day also report a significant decrease in inflammation due to arthritis.

8 Check Your Oil – Fat is an essential part of our diet, but good health depends on the use of the right kind of fat. When it comes to oil, remember that all oils are 100-percent fat. Be sure to choose expeller-pressed or cold-pressed oils, and keep in mind that canola and olive oil are the richest in monounsaturates, which is desirable. Grape seed oil is high in antioxidants, and flax oil is the highest in omega-3 essential fatty acid as discussed above. If you are trying to lose weight, consume fats in the packages

God placed them in — nuts, seeds, olives, and avocados — and you'll do better. In every case, avoid hydrogenated oils, as they contain harmful trans fatty acids.

9 Bone up on Calcium – Available from many sources, it is important to get enough calcium. Dark leafy greens like kale, collards, and turnip greens provide the best source, but almonds, sesame seeds, figs, and carob powder are rich in calcium as well. Arugula is a spicy herb that is higher in calcium than any other cultivated green, and it is delicious in salads. Vitamin D is needed for proper assimilation of calcium, so take a daily 30-minute walk in the sunshine to get your daily dose.

10 Shun the Sugar – Keep your intake of even healthy sweets to a minimum, serving desserts only a couple days per week. Whenever possible, use whole-food sweeteners like dates or other fresh or dried fruits. Check out the *Carob Pudding* and the *Banana Date Cookies*. They are plenty sweet but have no refined sugar. Sweet!

11 The Berry Best to You! – Strawberries, blueberries, blackberries: all kinds of berries are chock-full of antioxidants, anthocyanins to be specific. Scientists have learned that berries contribute to the prevention of everything from heart disease to cancer to age-related brain decline, and they also contain fiber, folate, and significant amounts of vitamin C. So have a berry merry time at breakfast, and include them in desserts like *Blackberry Cobbler*.

12 A Time to Eat, a Time to Drink – The right foods eaten at the right time provide optimum assimilation of nutrients and the best safeguard against disease. For the most favorable digestion, refrain from drinking with meals any more than one-half cup of liquid. Eat well at breakfast, and wait at least five hours before eating lunch, being sure to drink several glasses of water between meals. A light evening meal can be taken five hours later, though for many, no supper is preferable as to give the digestive system a good rest. To encourage weight loss, adopt a two-meal-a-day program by omitting supper. You'll be thrilled with the results!

If the name of a recipe is *italicized* within the text of this book, it indicates that it is a *Total Vegetarian* recipe that can be easily found in the index. A nutritional analysis is also provided for each recipe. These are approximate values. If a nutrient value differs from one given for a recipe in the *StepFast Resource Guide*, the value given in *The Total Vegetarian Cookbook* is more accurate.

Weight Control: Simple Savvy

We all know that when we burn more calories than we consume, we lose weight and, indeed — many have been able to trim down for a time through various dietary plans. However, keeping lost weight off is often a different matter. Clearly then, making permanent adjustments in dietary and lifestyle habits is the key to permanent weight loss. Confronting this reality is usually such great fear of the self-denial that will be required that indulgence is most often the victor, again and again.

Filled with frustration and discouragement, this is a battle I fought myself for years. That is why I am so excited to share with you the keys to controlling your appetite. These keys will lead not only to permanent weight loss, but they will also reduce the risk of heart disease, stroke, diabetes, depression, cancer, and other autoimmune diseases. The keys to weight control encompass all the *StepFast* principles, and they are incorporated here in a daily schedule.

1 A successful day starts the night before. Go to bed early enough to sleep eight to nine hours. Between 9:00 and 10:30 is an ideal bedtime for most people.

2 Before you go to sleep, cast your cares aside and think of events of the day for which you are thankful. A thankful heart does much to provide encouragement. In fact, "A merry heart doeth good like a medicine!" (Proverbs 17:22).

3 Rise early and drink one quart of warm water. Adding fresh lemon juice to the water enhances its cleansing ability.

4 Spend time reading the Bible and in prayer. Ask God to give you the strength to stick with your new lifestyle. Expect Him to do it and He will!

5 Take a brisk walk outdoors. You might need to start with 20 to 30 minutes and work up to 40 to 60 minutes. You can also choose to walk with a partner or allow Jesus to be your walking partner and continue your morning prayer while you walk. Enjoy the blessings of nature as you walk.

6 Eat a high-fiber, total vegetarian breakfast. This meal should include raw fruit, a whole-grain or legume entrée, as well as some nuts, nut butter, or a recipe made with nuts or seeds. It is important to include some high-fat food in order to feel satisfied and not get hungry between meals. This meal should consist of 600 to 700 calories. Do not have a beverage with your meal; drink water up to 30 minutes before eating and resume drinking water an hour later.

7 During the morning do not snack; however, you should drink three eight-ounce glasses of water. If you feel hungry, drink more water!

8 Enjoy another whole-foods vegan meal for lunch, being sure to include a large raw salad, one or two cooked vegetables, and an entrée made from legumes and whole grains. Remember, no beverage with your meal. Eat well; however, be sure not to overeat. This meal should consist of 500 to 600 calories. After lunch, go for a 10- to 15-minute stroll outdoors, breathing deeply while you walk.

9 During the afternoon, drink 2 to 3 more glasses of water. No snacks.

10 Change your pace in the evening. Do something physical if your daytime work is mostly sedentary, or vice versa. Work in some family or social time. Drink one more glass of water.

11 Eat a very light evening meal or skip supper altogether. Choose foods for this meal that are very low in fat, such as fruit, salads, and low-fat crackers. *Pita Chips* are a good choice. This meal should consist of only about 200 to 300 calories and should conclude several hours before you retire for the evening. A better choice than having supper would be to exercise!

12 Early to bed, early to rise!

Following this simple program, you will be able to enjoy a wide variety of delicious recipes and lose weight gradually and permanently.

Because you will have two generous meals, you will not feel deprived, nor will you be hungry. Many mistake thirst for hunger; if you feel hungry, drink water or herb tea. May you be blessed as you shed pounds, feel more energized, and begin to enjoy better health!

"Beloved, I wish above all things that thou mayest prosper and be in health, even as thy soul prospereth."
—3 John 2

Special Ingredients

Sometimes total vegetarian cookery calls for special ingredients with which the average cook might not be familiar. Every attempt has been made to keep such special ingredients to a minimum, but a few are required. Listed below are some of these unique ingredients included in *The Total Vegetarian Cookbook* recipes. Following the description of each is a symbol indicating where you can purchase the item. 🍎 indicates the item is likely to be found at a natural foods market or health food store, and 🛒 indicates that the item might be purchased at a grocery store. Some natural foods might need to be purchased from online vendors. Be sure to visit www.totalvegetarian.com, where some ingredients are offered for your convenience.

Almond Butter – A nut butter like peanut butter, but made with roasted almonds. My favorite is produced by Zinke's Almond Orchard. 🍎

Bakon Yeast – Similar to nutritional yeast flakes, Bakon yeast is torula yeast with a natural hickory smoke flavor. Gives a wonderful "real southern" flavor to cooked greens. 🍎

Bragg Liquid Aminos – This unfermented alternative to soy sauce is lower in sodium and has a mild, delicious, and somewhat "meaty" flavor. 🍎

Carob Powder – While there might be validity to deriving some health benefit from dark chocolate, the amount of fat and sugar needed to make it palatable nearly, if not completely, cancels it out. Possessing a flavor and appearance similar to chocolate, carob is actually a legume that is naturally sweet and thus requires less added sweetener. My experience with carob is that "it all depends on the recipe," and those presented in *The Total Vegetarian Cookbook* have passed many taste tests! 🍎

Carob Chips – Similar to chocolate chips, these tasty little morsels are made with carob powder and consequently require less sweetener than their look-alike. They do contain saturated fat, however, and could be replaced in any recipe with raisins for a healthier alternative. 🍎

Cashews – Cashews are soft and blend easily with water into a smooth cream. They should be purchased raw for cooking, whole or in pieces, and rinsed thoroughly as they can contain impurities. 🍎

Chicken-style Seasoning – A savory seasoning that gives gravies, tofu, or SoyCurls a delicious chicken-like flavor. McKay's Chicken-style Seasoning is available commercially, but this recipe is easy to mix and keeps well:

> 1 cup nutritional yeast flakes
> 1 tablespoon onion powder
> 2¼ teaspoons paprika
> 1½ teaspoons celery seed
> 1 tablespoon salt
> 1½ teaspoons sage
> 1½ teaspoons thyme
> 1½ teaspoons garlic powder
> ¾ teaspoon marjoram
> 1 tablespoon parsley flakes
> 1 tablespoon turbinado sugar
>
> Combine all ingredients and mix in dry blender. Store in a closed container.

Chili Powder – Hot chilies are irritating to the digestive tract. This "No Alarm" Chili Powder recipe is a healthy alternative to regular chili powder. An occasional dash of cayenne can be used for those who prefer a hotter chili, but it should be used in extreme moderation.

8 bay leaves
½ cup paprika
¼ cup parsley flakes
1 teaspoon garlic powder
1½ tablespoons onion powder
1½ tablespoons sweet basil
4 tablespoons oregano leaves
1½ teaspoons cumin

Blend all ingredients in a dry blender, being sure to blend bay leaves well. Store in air-tight container.

Coconut Milk – Studies now show that coconut oil might aid in lowering cholesterol and in normalizing thyroid function, so coconut milk may also be helpful. All my recipes that use this ingredient call not for the lite variety, but for the full-fat canned coconut milk, which produces incredible flavor and texture.

Curry Powder, Mild – A combination of a number of herbs and spices, curry powder is usually quite hot. Here's a recipe you can keep on hand that adds a pungent flavor without the hot, harsh spices.

1 tablespoon coriander
2 teaspoons cumin
2 tablespoons celery seed
1 teaspoon garlic powder
1½ tablespoons turmeric
½ teaspoon ground cardamom
1 tablespoon onion powder
12 bay leaves (optional)

Grind all ingredients in coffee mill or dry blender. If using bay leaves, be sure all leaf fragments are ground very fine. If omitting this ingredient, the curry powder may be mixed in a bowl with a spoon.

Date Sugar – Dried dates are crushed to produce this granulated form of dates. Though an expensive alternative to refined sugar, it is a very tasty whole-food sweetener.

Dulse – A seaweed product that is low in sodium and rich in trace minerals, granulated dulse is very palatable and an excellent alternative to salt, especially when sprinkled on vegetables. It does have a slight fishy taste, so experiment and use it sparingly at first.

Ener-G Baking Powder – Conventional baking powder (sodium bicarbonate and tartaric acid) is high in sodium, robs B vitamins when assimilated, is irritating to the digestive tract, might contribute to the formation of gallstones, and often contains aluminum. While Rumford baking powder is aluminum-free, it still has all the risk factors of other brands. Ener-G baking powder is a combination of citric acid and calcium carbonate, and when used in baking, produces the most readily absorbed form of calcium, calcium citrate. It is moisture activated and requires about double the amount of regular baking powder. Ener-G baking products are available in health food stores, at Adventist Book and Health Food stores at (800) 765-6955, or can be ordered from Ener-G Foods, Inc. at (800) 331-5222 or www.ener-g.com

Instant Clear Jel – Also known as modified food starch, this pre-cooked cornstarch instantly thickens puddings and salad dressings when sprinkled into swirling liquid in a running blender.

Lemon Juice – Fresh is always best, but a convenient alternative is pure, reconstituted lemon juice that can be found in the freezer section.

Maltitol – A sugar alcohol that is not absorbed by the body, maltitol is used to produce imitation honey and syrups. It can be used occasionally in small amounts. Excessive use might cause gastrointestinal problems.

Nutritional Yeast Flakes – Loaded with B vitamins, nutritional yeast flakes give a cheesy flavor and a nutritional boost to dairy-free cheese recipes.

Real Salt – This is the brand name of a product that is 98 percent sodium chloride, but it also contains 50 trace minerals including calcium, potassium, sulphur, phosphorus, manganese, copper, iodine, and zinc. Real Salt is recommended for all recipes that call for salt.

Roma – This roasted grain beverage resembles coffee, but contains no caffeine or tannin. A key ingredient in carob recipes and a delicious warm beverage on a cold winter's night. A similar product, Postum, is available at the grocery store.

Soy Curls – A whole soybean meat substitute, Soy Curls are as versatile as chicken and beef. Included in *The Total Vegetarian Cookbook* are a number of delicious recipes, but with a little creativity, an endless number of recipes could be developed. Available from Butler Foods at (503) 879-5005, at www.totalvegetarian.com, and some natural foods markets.

Soymilk Powder – Convenient for travel, soymilk powder is also used to add richness to some recipes.

Stevia – A no-carbohydrate herbal sweetener that is much sweeter than sugar and provides a healthy alternative. I encourage you to experiment using half-refined sweetener and a small amount of stevia in puddings and whipped topping. SweetLeaf Stevia Plus is the brand I recom-mend.

Sucanat – The name for this dehydrated sugar cane juice is derived from "sugar cane natural." A simple carbohydrate, Sucanat does have slightly more nutritive value than white or turbinado sugar.

Tahini – A purée of sesame seeds, tahini is a seed butter similar to nut butters like peanut and almond butter. Its slightly bitter taste makes a perfect ingredient for mock cheese recipes, adding a sharp cheese flavor.

Tofu – Studies have demonstrated that including tofu in the diet might help prevent heart disease, osteoporosis, and breast and prostate cancer and can reduce menopausal symptoms such as mood swings and hot flashes. Low in fat and cholesterol-free, tofu can also contribute significantly to an effective weight-loss program. Providing high-quality protein, tofu, like soybeans, contains isoflavones, including a powerful anti-cancer agent called genestein, as well as other phytochemicals.

Somewhat like cottage cheese, tofu, which is soybean curd, comes in different degrees of firmness. Most of my recipes call for fresh, water-packed firm or extra-firm tofu since this consistency contains less water and more nutrition. Silken tofu, which comes in an aseptic box, is perfect for puddings or mousse.

Though recognized by many as a "super food," tofu often receives a reluctant reception. Many have had an unfortunate introduction to tofu, and it is my mission to help people recover from their "tofu phobia!" The health benefits and ease of preparation of this convenient, nutrient-dense food make it way too good to write off as weird or unsavory. With the recipes you find in *The Total Vegetarian Cookbook,* I believe you'll find that tofu can be incredibly delicious!

Turbinado Sugar – Also known as raw sugar, turbinado has just a few nutrients, but it provides all the simple carbohydrate grams of regular granulated sugar.

Vegeburger – Available canned or frozen, this crumbled hamburger substitute is made from soy protein or wheat gluten.

Vegenaise – A soy-based, vegan mayonnaise that contains vinegar and lemon juice. Homemade Tofu Mayonnaise contains no vinegar and would be preferable, but Vegenaise can be used for the sake of convenience.

Vegesal – A blend of salt and vegetable crystals with a bit of kelp added, Vegesal is much lower in sodium than table salt. One teaspoon contains 1420 mg of sodium, as compared to 2400 mg in salt, which includes sea salt. Real Salt and Herbemare are also recommended.

Recipes
Beverages

Carrot juice recipe on page 31

Raspberry Zinger Punch

A refreshing beverage that is pretty in the glass and not too sweet. Perfect for wedding receptions!

Ingredients

3 quarts water
8 Red Zinger tea bags
12-ounce can raspberry white
  grape juice concentrate

Per 8 ounces:
  Calories 60
  Protein .5 g
  Carbohydrates 14 g
  Fiber 0 g
  Fat 0 g
  Sodium 4 mg

Steps

1 Bring 1 quart of water to a boil. Add tea bags and let it steep for 5 minutes.

2 Add juice concentrate and remaining 2 quarts of water and stir.

3 Chill and serve with orange slices floating in a punch bowl or with juice and orange slices frozen in gelatin molds afloat.

Makes 13 servings.

COOK'S TIP

If a lack of refrigerator space makes chilling the punch a challenge, use only 2½ quarts of water, then add a tray of ice cubes just before serving.

Carrot Juice

Supplementing your diet with fresh vegetable juices is an excellent way to give yourself a nutritional boost. Juicing carrots and other vegetables produces a beverage that tastes great and is chock-full of vitamins and minerals. Here's one time to be sure to use organically grown produce. Although carrot juice is full of nutrients, including naturally occurring sugar, if conventionally grown produce is used, you'll also get a concentration of pesticides. So, go organic!

Ingredients

1 pound organically grown carrots

Per 8 ounces:
    Calories 95
    Protein 2.2 g
    Carbohydrates 22 g
    Fiber 1 g
    Fat .3 g
    Sodium 70 mg

Steps

1 Scrub carrots well. Cut off tops.

2 Extract juice from carrots using a Champion Juicer or another type of juice extractor. Drink immediately. For optimal digestion, swish the juice in your mouth as you drink it.

Makes about 1 cup.

"The first wealth is health."
    —Ralph Waldo Emerson

Green Smoothie

Absolutely the best way to get your calcium and other important minerals.

Ingredients

2 cups fresh pineapple chunks
2 cups fresh parsley, packed
½ cup water
4 ice cubes
5 prinkle of stevia powder
2 tablespoons pineapple juice
  concentrate (optional)

Per cup:
  Calories 50
  Protein 1.7 g
  Carbohydrates 12.5 g
  Fiber 2.5 g
  Fat 0 g
  Sodium 25 mg

Steps

1 Include the core of the pineapple when preparing it for the smoothie.

2 Combine all ingredients in blender and blend until smooth.

Makes 3 cups.

COOK'S TIP

You also can use kale, spinach, or young collards for this mineral-rich drink. Better yet, use lambsquarters, often considered a weed, right out of your yard or garden.

Soymilk

Soymilk is available in almost every grocery store these days, with options of plain, vanilla, and unsweetened — even carob and chocolate! Yet homemade soymilk is even more nutritious in that you can choose to keep the fiber and control the amount and type of sweetener used. Additionally, commercial soymilk can cost as much as $.50 per serving, while the homemade version will cost only a dime per serving!

Ingredients

½ cup dry soybeans
3–4 pitted dates
Water
¼ teaspoon salt

Per 1 cup:
  Calories 99
  Protein 8.5 g
  Carbohydrates 8 g
  Fiber 3.3 g
  Fat 4.5 g
  Sodium 76 mg

Steps

1 Cover soybeans in a medium-sized bowl with 2 cups water. Soak overnight or at least five hours. Drain and place in a large saucepan with the dates and 2 cups fresh water.

2 Bring to a boil and allow it to boil gently for 5 minutes.

3 Drain and combine with 2 cups fresh water, dates, and salt. Blend until smooth.

4 Add water or ice cubes to make one quart or to desired consistency. One tray of ice is equal to 2 cups of water. Strain if desired.

Makes 1 quart.

COOK'S TIP

Soybeans can be soaked ahead of time and stored in the freezer in plastic bags in **1**-cup portions. Rinse them with hot water and proceed with the recipe.

Sweet Nut Milk

There's no need for sugary cereals with this delicious nut milk poured over granola and other wholesome cereals.

Ingredients

1 quart water
⅔ cup rinsed, raw cashews
  or almonds
4 pitted dates
¼ teaspoon salt
½ teaspoon lemon juice

Per ½ cup:
  Calories 105 g
  Protein 3.1 g
  Carbohydrates 7.3 g
  Fiber .8 g
  Fat 7.4 g
  Sodium 69 mg

Steps

1 Place nuts, dates, and salt in blender with 1 cup of the water and blend until smooth. Add remaining water and blend again to mix.

2 Serve immediately with hot cereal. Otherwise, store in the refrigerator for later use.

3 Shake well before each use.

Makes 4½ cups.

COOK'S TIP

For "unsweetened" nut milk, decrease sweetener to one date or ½ teaspoon of honey. Dairy milk is not exactly sweet, but its flavor is not flat either. The taste of milk is actually a combination of three tastes: sweet, sour, and salty. That's why even this "unsweetened" nut milk requires a small amount of sweetener to achieve the desired flavor.

Tropical Milk

Cow's milk is the perfect food for baby cows! Dairy milk is linked to many diseases in humans, from juvenile diabetes and allergies to digestive problems and degenerative diseases. This alternative is delicious.

Ingredients

13.5-ounce can coconut milk
1 tablespoon sweetener
½ teaspoon vanilla extract
⅛ teaspoon salt
Water to make 2 quarts

Per ½ cup:
  Calories 50
  Protein .5 g
  Carbohydrates 1.5 g
  Fiber 0 g
  Fat 5 g
  Sodium 45 mg

Steps

1 Blend all ingredients in a blender, adding water gradually. Decrease water and add ice cubes if chilled milk is desired.

2 Store in refrigerator.

Makes 16 servings.

Hot Carob

Nothing beats a hot drink like this one on a chilly evening. Gather around the fire and enjoy a cup!

Ingredients

2 cups vanilla soymilk
1½ teaspoons carob powder
1 tablespoon honey
¼ teaspoon stevia powder
½ teaspoon vanilla extract
Dash of salt

Per 8 ounces:
    Calories 165
    Protein 9.5 g
    Carbohydrates 23 g
    Fiber 3.5 g
    Fat 5 g
    Sodium 110 mg

Steps

1 Briefly blend all ingredients in a blender.

2 Heat in a saucepan over medium heat, just until steaming.

3 Serve hot.

Makes 2 servings.

Cappuccino

The coffee craze has reached America from across the Atlantic! With this easy recipe, you can skip the coffee and have the added benefit of soymilk. Enjoy a small serving with dessert.

Ingredients

2 cups vanilla soymilk
2 tablespoons maple syrup
2 teaspoons powdered coffee substitute (Roma or Postum)
½ teaspoon vanilla extract

Per ½ cup:
    Calories 60
    Protein 4.5 g
    Carbohydrates 12.5 g
    Fiber 1.5 g
    Fat 2.5 g
    Sodium 15 mg

Steps

1 Briefly blend all ingredients in a blender.

2 Serve hot or chilled.

Makes 4 servings.

"You must take time for your health, or you will take time for disease."
—Agatha Thrash, MD

Breakfast

Baked Oatmeal recipe on page 50

Stoplight Tofu

Red, yellow, and green bell peppers are often sold together. One package I saw was cylindrical and looked like a traffic light! These peppers are chock-full of vitamin C and add an appealing array of color. This breakfast recipe is sure to give you the green light for a great day!

Ingredients

1 small onion
½ green bell pepper
½ yellow bell pepper
½ red bell pepper
14 ounces fresh, firm tofu
2 teaspoons chicken-style seasoning
¼ teaspoon turmeric
1½ teaspoons olive oil
    or 1 tablespoon of water
2 teaspoons parsley flakes
Salt to taste

Per 1 cup:
    Calories 185
    Protein 16.5 g
    Carbohydrates 11 g
    Fiber 3.5 g
    Fat 10 g
    Sodium 565 mg

Steps

1 Peel and slice onion in half, then into thin slices. Cut peppers into 2 x ½-inch strips; slice tofu into ¼ x 1-inch squares.

2 Sauté onions and peppers in oil or steam in water for 3 minutes.

3 Add tofu and seasonings and stir to coat. Cover and steam for 5 more minutes.

Makes 4 servings.

Scrambled Tofu

Serve Oven Roasted Potatoes, *page 56,* Scrambled Tofu, *and sliced tomatoes for a savory breakfast treat that provides a great nutritional foundation for a productive day!*

Ingredients

1 teaspoon salt
1 tablespoon parsley flakes
    or chopped fresh parsley
14 ounces fresh, firm tofu
¼ cup rinsed, raw cashews
2 tablespoons nutritional
    yeast flakes
¼ teaspoon turmeric or
    2 tablespoons cooked carrots
¼ teaspoon garlic powder
½ teaspoon lemon juice
2 teaspoons onion powder
½ cup water

Per ½ cup:
    Calories 240
    Protein 19.9 g
    Carbohydrates 10.8 g
    Fiber 4.1 g
    Fat 15.4 g
    Sodium 600 mg

"Is tasteless food eaten without salt, or is there flavor in the white of an egg? I refuse to touch it; such food makes me ill."
    —Job 6:6, 7 (NIV)

Steps

1 Crumble tofu into fine pieces in a non-stick skillet. A potato masher works well for this. Sprinkle with parsley and ¼ teaspoon of the salt. Heat in the skillet about 10 minutes until dry.

2 Blend the remaining ingredients, including the remaining ¾ teaspoon of salt, in a blender until smooth. Pour the blended mixture over tofu in skillet and scramble over medium heat until desired consistency.

Makes 4 servings.

Simple Scrambled Tofu

Tasty and quick when you're in a hurry. No blender necessary.

Ingredients

14 ounces fresh, firm tofu
1 medium onion, chopped
1 teaspoon olive oil or
    2 tablespoons water
1 tablespoon chicken-style
    seasoning
1 teaspoon onion powder
2 teaspoons parsley flakes
½ teaspoon salt or to taste

Per ½ cup:
    Calories 165
    Protein 16 g
    Carbohydrates 8 g
    Fiber 2.5 g
    Fat 9 g
    Sodium 300 mg

Steps

1 Sauté onion in olive oil or water.

2 Cube or break tofu in pieces into non-stick skillet.

3 Add remaining seasonings and stir, allowing tofu to slightly brown over medium heat.

Makes 4 servings.

"Risk for disease goes up dramatically when even a little animal protein is added to the diet."

—T. Colin Campbell, PhD, author, The China Study

Chipped Tofu

This delicious entrée is featured on the menu for guests of the Lifestyle Center of America. It is nutrient-dense and has a stick-to-your-ribs quality that makes it easy to follow a "no snacking" policy the rest of the day.

Ingredients

14 ounces fresh, firm tofu
2 cups water
2½ tablespoons chicken-style
    seasoning
½ cup rinsed, raw cashews
1½ tablespoons cornstarch
1 tablespoon onion powder
    or ¼ cup chopped onion
1½ tablespoons Bragg Liquid Aminos
2 cups additional water

Per ½ cup:
   Calories 165
   Protein 10.5 g
   Carbohydrates 8.9 g
   Fiber 1.5 g
   Fat 11 g
   Sodium 415 mg

Steps

1 In a saucepan, combine 2 cups water with 1½ tablespoons of the chicken-style seasoning.

2 Slice tofu into ¼ inch cubes. Add cubed tofu and boil for 20 minutes. Drain and set aside.

3 Pour 1 cup water into another saucepan and bring to a boil.

4 In a blender, combine remaining 1 cup water with remaining tablespoon of chicken-style seasoning, cashews, onion powder, Bragg Liquid Aminos, and cornstarch. Process on high speed until smooth. Pour into saucepan with boiling water and cook until thick.

5 Add boiled tofu and stir briefly. Serve over toast, rice, or pasta.

Makes 8 servings.

"Living a healthy lifestyle will only deprive you of poor health, lethargy, and fat."

—Jill Johnson

Overnight Waffles

A hearty meal disguised as a waffles breakfast.

Ingredients

¾ cup dry soybeans
½ cup brown rice
2 pitted dates
½ cup cornmeal
¾ teaspoon salt
1 teaspoon vanilla
2½ cups water

Per serving:
    Calories 200
    Protein 10.5 g
    Carbohydrates 29 g
    Fiber 4 g
    Fat 5.5 g
    Sodium 290 mg

Steps

1 Cover dry soybeans, rice, and dates with 4 cups water in a large bowl. Allow to soak overnight and drain water. They will approximately double in size.

2 Combine soybeans, rice, and dates and place in blender with remaining ingredients.

3 Blend until smooth.

4 Bake in preheated waffle iron for 8-9 minutes.

5 Serve with fresh peaches or strawberries and *Berry Fruit Sauce,* page 189.

Makes 12 serving.

Belgian Waffles

You won't have to call anyone to breakfast twice after the aroma of these waffles wafts through the house. You will be amazed how light and golden brown with crispy edges these are, without eggs or baking powder. The heat of the waffle iron does the leavening.

Ingredients

4 ¾ cups water
¾ teaspoon salt
¼ cup nuts or seeds
½ cup cornmeal
⅛ cup date pieces
3 cups rolled oats

Per waffle:
  Calories 330
  Protein 12 g
  Carbohydrates 42 g
  Fiber 7.5 g
  Fat 14 g
  Sodium 300 mg

Steps

1 Blend all ingredients except the oats, starting with 2 cups of water.

2 Add oats and 2 ¼ cups of the remaining water and blend until smooth. Let the batter sit for 3 minutes.

3 Pour 1¼ cups of batter onto preheated, oil-sprayed Belgian waffle iron, not allowing batter to come completely to sides. Bake for 10 to 12 minutes or until golden brown.

4 Add another ¼ cup of the water to batter and blend again. You will see batter thickens as it sits. Pour the second waffle in the iron, then add the final ¼ cup of water and blend again. Repeat process. Waffle iron may get hotter during the process, so watch carefully! Cooking time might need to be decreased.

Makes 6 waffles.

COOK'S TIP

Use a regular waffle iron for thinner waffles. Waffles can be made ahead of time and frozen for later use. Just pop them in the toaster!

Variation: For sesame oat waffles, sprinkle waffle iron with 1 teaspoon sesame seeds, pour batter and sprinkle top with sesame seeds before baking.

Stuffed French Toast

A great take-along breakfast, these pitas resemble a fruit pie after baking. Our vacations always started early in the morning with a breakfast on the road of Stuffed French Toast, *dipped into individual cups of* Strawberry Jam. *The station owners never seemed to mind when I'd warm up an entire plastic bag full of these yummy breakfast treats in their microwave!*

Ingredients

¼ cup pitted dates
½ cup raw cashews
2 tablespoons rolled oats
1 cup water
¼ teaspoon salt (or less)
4 whole wheat pitas
13.5-ounce can pears, in juice

Per serving:
    Calories 160
    Protein 4.5 g
    Carbohydrates 22 g
    Fiber 3 g
    Fat 7 g
    Sodium 100 mg

Steps

1 Blend dates, cashews, salt, and water until very smooth and pour into a shallow dish.

2 Cut pita bread in half. Stuff with pears, flattening the pears as you stuff them into the pita pocket, and bring the opening of the pita back together as much as possible. Dip bread into batter, carefully covering the top well, not leaving finger prints!

3 Bake on baking sheet, ideally covered with parchment paper at 350° for 30 minutes.

4 Serve with *Berry Fruit Sauce,* page 189, or *Strawberry Jam,* page 190.

Makes 8 servings.

HEALTH TIP

An abundance of valuable fiber is found not only in whole grains, but also in fruits, vegetables, and legumes.

French Toast

The original recipe called for stale bread. In fact, the French, who apparently developed the recipe, call it "pain perdu" or "lost bread," bread that would otherwise be lost! But mercy intervenes and nothing is lost in this recipe, except the unwanted cholesterol.

Ingredients

¼ cup pitted dates
½ cup rinsed, raw cashews
1 cup water
¼ teaspoon salt (or less)
8 slices *Whole Wheat Bread,*
    page 57

Per slice:
    Calories 160
    Protein 5 g
    Carbohydrates 20 g
    Fiber 3 g
    Fat 8 g
    Sodium 210 mg

Steps

1 In the blender, blend dates, cashews, salt, and water until very smooth. Pour into a shallow dish and dip bread into batter.

2 Brown in a pre-heated, non-stick skillet over medium heat, or bake on a baking sheet at 350° for 30 minutes.

3 Serve with *Berry Fruit Sauce,* page 189, or simply with applesauce or fresh fruit. Delicious with peaches served on top!

Makes 8 slices.

Quick French Toast

It doesn't get any easier than this! Start with Whole Wheat Bread *and this recipe is wonderful.*

Ingredients

8 slices *Whole Wheat Bread,*
    page 57
Rich soymilk or nut milk

Per slice:
    Calories 80
    Protein 4 g
    Carbohydrates 13 g
    Fiber 2 g
    Fat 1.5 g
    Sodium 140 mg

Steps

1 Dip bread briefly in soymilk and brown slowly over medium-low heat in a non-stick skillet. Be sure the skillet is pre-heated.

2 Serve with apple sauce or *Berry Fruit Sauce,* page 189.

Makes 8 slices.

Crockpot Cereal

The absolute best way to get a wide variety of whole grains is with crockpot cookery. All grains have the same amino acids, but in varying amounts. Using a variety of grains will provide a more balanced nutrient profile. With the crockpot method, it's easy to incorporate grains that otherwise are hard to come by in a typical diet. Try some amaranth or quinoa for a great nutrient package and a welcomed change from oats. Other grains you can combine are: amaranth, quinoa, barley, wheat berries, oat groats, buckwheat, millet, and brown rice.

Ingredients

1 cup whole grain
3½ cups water
½ teaspoon salt

Per cup:
    Calories 195
    Protein 5 g
    Carbohydrates 33 g
    Fiber 5.5 g
    Fat 4.5 g
    Sodium 300 mg

Steps

1. Choose 1 to 3 whole grains and combine with remaining ingredients in a mini-crockpot (one quart). Cook overnight on low. One-quart crockpots have only one setting.

2. Add dried fruit after cooking, if desired.

3. Serve with soy or nut milk, fresh fruit, granola, ground flaxseed, and/or applesauce.

Makes 4 servings.

COOK'S TIP

Double or triple recipe for larger crockpot.

Fancy Crockpot Cereal

More taste, more nutrition, wonderful texture. If it's your turn to fix breakfast, do it in five minutes the night before!

Ingredients

⅓ cup wheat berries
⅓ cup oat groats or rolled oats
⅓ cup quinoa or millet
½ cup applesauce
¼ cup shredded coconut
½ teaspoon salt
1 teaspoon coriander
¼ cup chopped dried pineapple
    (optional)
3½ cups water

Per cup (without the dried
    pineapple and raisins):
    Calories 160
    Protein 4 g
    Carbohydrates 30 g
    Fiber 3.4 g
    Fat 3.4 g
    Sodium 300 mg

Steps

1 Combine all ingredients in a 1-quart crockpot and cook on low overnight.

2 Toss in a few raisins in the morning, if desired.

3 Serve with fresh fruit, granola, and soy or nut milk.

Makes 4 servings.

HEALTH TIP

For best digestion and assimilation of nutrients, eat fruit at one meal and vegetables at another.

Baked Oatmeal

This no-fuss recipe can be made the night before and baked just before breakfast. I like to add a cup of blueberries for a fruity punch of antioxidants!

Ingredients

3 cups rolled oats
¾ cup raisins or chopped dates
½ cup coconut, unsweetened
1 teaspoon salt
4½ cups water

Per ½ cup:
    Calories 170
    Protein 4.2 g
    Carbohydrates 24 g
    Fiber 4 g
    Fat 7.4 g
    Sodium 200 mg

Steps

1 Mix all ingredients in oil-sprayed 13 x 9-inch pan.

2 Bake uncovered at 350° for about 1 hour.

Makes 12 servings.

COOK'S TIP

To decrease baking time, use hot water in this recipe.

Charlie's Cran-Apple Granola

A love of certain ingredients can be the inspiration for a great recipe. That was true in Charlie's case; she's crazy about Craisins! And her recipe has gotten rave reviews.

Ingredients

7 cups quick oats
1 cup sliced almonds
1 cup chopped dried apples
1 cup dried cranberries
1 banana
1 cup pitted dates
⅓ cup Sucanat
    or turbinado sugar
¼ cup light olive oil
1 tablespoon vanilla extract
¾ cup water
1½ teaspoons salt

Per ½ cup:
    Calories 202
    Protein 5 g
    Carbohydrates 33.6 g
    Fiber 3.9 g
    Fat 6.3 g
    Sodium 151 mg

*"His compassions fail not.
They are new every morning;
Great is Your faithfulness."*

    —Lamentations 3:22, 23

Steps

1 Combine oats and almonds in a mixing bowl. Set dried fruit aside to add during the last 45 minutes of baking time.

2 Place remaining ingredients in blender and blend smooth. Pour over oats and almonds.

3 Using a plastic glove, mix both mixtures together with your hands. When thoroughly mixed, spread out on two cookie sheets covered with parchment paper or oil-sprayed.

4 Bake at 125°, with the oven setting on "warm," overnight or for two hours at 225°, stirring every 30 minutes. Add dried apples and cranberries. Store in airtight container.

Makes 24 servings.

Hi-Fiber Granola

Granola adds a wonderful crunch to hot cereal. Bake this overnight in a "slow" oven and breakfast will be ready when you wake up in the morning. The aroma will let you know!

Ingredients

2 ripe bananas
1 cup pitted dates
¾ cup water
6 cups old-fashioned rolled oats
1 cup wheat bran
½ cup ground flaxseed
1¼ teaspoons salt
1 cup chopped walnuts
1 cup chipped coconut

Per ½ cup:
  Calories 180
  Protein 5 g
  Carbohydrates 25.5 g
  Fiber 4.2 g
  Fat 7 g
  Sodium 140 mg

Steps

1 Heat dates and water together. Blend until smooth in blender with bananas and salt.

2 Combine remaining ingredients in a large bowl. Add blended mixture and, using plastic gloves, mix well with hands. It should stick together when grabbed by the handful.

3 Bake on two non-stick cookie sheets in the oven overnight at 125°, with the oven setting on "warm." In the morning, raise oven temperature to 200° for 30 minutes to brown slightly.

4 Serve over fruit or *Crockpot Cereal*, page 48, and add soy or nut milk, or use as a topping for pudding or banana smoothies.

Makes 24 servings.

COOK'S TIP

Bananas that have been frozen and thawed work well in this recipe. Keep some on hand in the freezer for granola *and* for smoothies!

Maple Walnut Granola

Rich but delicious, a little of this granola goes a long way. A great topping for pudding or smoothies.

Ingredients

1 cup pitted dates
¾ cup water
½ cup maple syrup
¼ cup light olive oil
2 teaspoons vanilla extract
2 teaspoons maple extract
1½ teaspoons salt
7 cups old fashioned rolled oats
1 cup unsweetened chipped
    coconut
1 cup walnuts, coarsely chopped
1 cup pecan meal
1 cup pumpkin or sunflower seeds

Per ½ cup:
    Calories 245
    Protein 9 g
    Carbohydrates 32 g
    Fiber 3 g
    Fat 10 g
    Sodium 130 mg

Steps

1 Heat dates and water in the microwave or in a saucepan until dates are soft. Place in the blender with maple syrup, oil, vanilla and maple extracts, and salt. Blend until smooth.

2 In a large bowl, combine all dry ingredients and pour in the blended mixture. Using plastic gloves, mix with your hands until the dry ingredients are well coated. Mixture should hold together when you squeeze a handful together.

3 Spread out on two cookie sheets covered with parchment paper or sprayed with oil.

4 Bake overnight at 125°, with the oven setting on "warm," or for 2 hours at 225°, stirring every 30 minutes.

Makes 27 servings.

HEALTH TIP

The high selenium content of Brazil nuts discourages the aging process! In just one ounce of these potassium-rich nuts, there are 840 mcg. of selenium. Replace walnuts with chopped Brazil nuts in granola from time to time and enjoy the benefits.

Breads & Such

Honey Wheat Bread

Made by hand or in a bread machine, this recipe seems to be foolproof. The molasses makes all the difference!

Ingredients

1¼ cups warm water
1 tablespoon honey
1 tablespoon molasses
2 teaspoons dry yeast *
1 teaspoon salt
1½ tablespoons oil
1½ cups unbleached white flour
1½ cups whole wheat flour
¼ cup additional flour
    for kneading

Per slice, 1/16 of a loaf:
    Calories 99
    Protein 3.2 g
    Carbohydrates 20.5 g
    Fiber 2 g
    Fat .8 g
    Sodium 148 mg

*"Jesus said to them,
'I am the bread of life.
He who comes to Me
shall never hunger, and
he who believes in Me
shall never thirst.'"*

—John 6:35

Steps

1 Put the warm water in a large mixing bowl. Add the honey and molasses and stir until they are dissolved.

2 Sprinkle in the yeast and stir. Let this mixture rest until the yeast comes to the top of the mixture, a matter of only two or three minutes. This step is to "proof" the yeast, making sure it has leavening power.

3 Add the salt and the oil and stir, making sure that all ingredients are mixed well. Add half of the flour and beat the batter for 3 to 5 minutes.

4 Add the rest of the flour gradually. You need less on a dry day, more on a damp day. Use an extra ¼ cup flour if it is needed to absorb the liquid in forming a ball of dough.

5 Place the dough ball on a surface sprinkled with flour. Rub a little flour on your hands and proceed to knead. Fold the dough toward you. Using the heels of your hands, push the dough away from you with a rolling motion. Do not be afraid to use a firm touch. Swing the dough a quarter turn around.

6 Repeat the kneading technique until the dough is smooth and elastic, 8 to 10 minutes. If the dough becomes sticky, sprinkle the surface with a small amount of flour and rub your hands with flour again. The dough has been kneaded enough when it is pressed with a finger and it springs back.

Recipe continues on next page …

7 Place the ball of dough in a large oiled mixing bowl and cover it with a damp cloth. Let it rise in a warm place, free from draft until it doubles in bulk, about an hour.

8 Test for readiness by pressing the dough carefully with your thumb. If the hole remains, the bread has risen enough.

9 Push your fist into the center of the dough, pull the edges to the center, and turn it over. Cover the dough and let it rest for 15 minutes. This resting encourages development of the gluten, the protein part of the flour.

10 Flatten out the dough. Fold each side to the middle, the width being the length of the bread pan. Start at the top and roll toward you, pressing with each turn to get out the air bubbles, which make the texture of the loaf coarse.

11 Place the formed loaf into an oiled loaf pan, 8½ x 4½ x 2½ inches in size, with the seam side of the loaf on the bottom of the pan. Cover with a damp cloth and let rise in a warm place free from drafts until it has doubled in bulk, about one hour. The bread is ready for the oven when the dough just begins to go over the edge of the pan.

12 Bake in oven preheated to 350° for 40 minutes or until brown on the bottom.

13 Remove from pan at once. If the loaf has not browned well on the outside, return it to the oven set on a cookie sheet until browned nicely. Set on wire rack to cool.

 * If using a bread machine, decrease yeast to 1¼ teaspoons.

Makes 1 loaf.

Whole Wheat Bread

100-percent Whole Wheat Bread is a hearty, but flavorful, bread.

Ingredients

4 cups warm water
⅓ cup honey
2 tablespoons dry yeast
9–9½ cups whole wheat flour *
¼ cup oil
¼ cup gluten flour
1 tablespoon salt

* Flour amount may very due to
moisture variations in the flour and air.

Per slice:
    Calories 100
    Protein 3.5 g
    Carbohydrates 19.5 g
    Fiber 3 g
    Fat 1.5 g
    Sodium 150 mg

COOK'S TIP

The gluten flour adds to the
meshwork of the bread dough,
allowing it to rise well. Often
called "vital gluten," gluten
flour is sold in natural foods
markets.

Steps

1 In a large bowl, stir together water,
honey, yeast, and 2 cups of the whole
wheat flour; let bubble in warm place 15 to
20 minutes to "proof" the yeast.

2 Stir in oil and salt. Gradually add about
6 cups* of whole wheat flour until it
becomes difficult to stir.

3 Turn dough out onto floured surface and
add 1 to 1½ cups more flour. Knead
well until texture is correct. Dough should
spring back when lightly pressed.

4 Put the dough back into the bowl, cover,
and let it rise in warm place until about
double in bulk.

5 Punch down and knead briefly in the
bowl. Cut into three equal pieces. Knead
each piece on lightly floured counter.

6 Shape into loaves and place in oiled
pans, 8½ x 4½ x 2½ inches in size.
Cover and let it rise again in pans in warm
place until not quite doubled in size.

7 Bake in oven preheated to 350° for 40
to 45 minutes. Remove from pans and
allow to cool on a wire rack.

8 Allow to "rest" 24 hours so byproducts
of yeast fermentation dissipate.

Makes 3 loaves.

Spoon Bread

Southern-style spoon bread was my childhood favorite. This vegan version has a rich cornmeal flavor and a wonderful creamy texture.

Ingredients

1½ cups water
1½ cups soymilk
¾ cup cornmeal
1 teaspoon honey
½ teaspoon salt
2 tablespoons light olive oil

Per ½ cup:
  Calories 80
  Protein 2 g
  Carbohydrates 7.5 g
  Fiber 1 g
  Fat 4.5 g
  Sodium 250 mg

COOK'S TIP

This recipe is especially good served with a vegan buttery spread like Smart Balance Light.

Steps

1 Preheat oven to 400°.

2 In a medium saucepan, combine water and soymilk. Place over medium-high heat.

3 Immediately, sprinkle in cornmeal, stirring constantly with a whisk. Add honey, salt, and oil and continue to whisk over the heat until thickened.

4 Pour the mixture into an oiled 8 x 8-inch baking dish or round baking dish of similar size.

5 Bake for 25 to 30 minutes or just until set. Allow to cool just slightly. The spoon bread will become firmer as it cools. The texture is very nice when it cools completely and is reheated.

Makes 8 servings.

Soy Corn Muffins

Serve these muffins with black-eyed peas, Fresh Collard Greens, *page 165, and* Sweet Potato Soufflé, *page 167, southern style! These muffins are hearty but really delicious.*

Ingredients

2 cups soaked soybeans
    (1 cup dry)
2 cups cornmeal, unrefined
2¼ cups water
1½ teaspoons salt
¼ cup quick oats
2 tablespoons honey
½ teaspoon onion powder

Per muffin:
    Calories 160
    Protein 8 g
    Carbohydrates 26 g
    Fiber 4.5 g
    Fat 4 g
    Sodium 290 mg

Steps

1 Preheat oven to 400°.

2 For 2 cups soaked soybeans, soak 1 cup dry soybeans in 3 cups water overnight or for 5 hours. The beans may be soaked in advance and stored in plastic bags in the freezer.

3 Combine all ingredients except the cornmeal in the blender and blend until smooth. Pour into a bowl and add cornmeal. Mix well.

4 Spoon batter into oiled muffin tin, filling to the top to make 12 muffins. A pre-heated, oil-sprayed cast iron corn pone pan also works well.

5 Bake for 30 minutes and serve hot. Store any leftover muffins in the refrigerator. Steam to reheat.

Makes 1 dozen.

COOK'S TIP

The soybeans add nutrition and act as a leavening agent, so no eggs or baking powder are needed. Be sure to keep some frozen soaked soybeans on hand so you'll have everything you need for this recipe.

Blueberry Muffins

A nice addition to breakfast or brunch, these muffins are whole grain and contain antioxidant morsels bursting with flavor. Little refined sweetener is needed with the natural sweetness of the pineapple.

Ingredients

¼ cup almond butter
   or light olive oil
20-ounce can crushed pineapple
   with juice
2 teaspoons vanilla extract
⅔ cup honey
2¾ cups whole wheat pastry flour
½ teaspoon salt
3 tablespoons Ener-G baking
   powder or 1½ tablespoons
   Rumford Baking Powder.
2 cups blueberries, fresh or frozen

Per muffin:
   Calories 120
   Protein 2 g
   Carbohydrates 24 g
   Fiber 2.5 g
   Fat 2 g
   Sodium 60 mg

COOK'S TIP

Pastry flour is made from spring wheat berries and is somewhat finer than regular whole wheat flour. If only regular whole wheat is available, use 1 cup unbleached white flour and 1½ cups whole wheat.

Steps

1 Preheat oven to 375°.

2 Blend almond butter or oil, pineapple, vanilla and honey in blender until smooth.

3 Combine unsifted flour, salt, and baking powder in a large bowl and mix well.

4 Pour wet mixture into dry ingredients and mix well but quickly, being careful not to stir out bubbles.

5 Fold in blueberries. If berries are frozen, rinse briefly under warm water before adding.

6 Line muffin tin with paper baking cups. Spray the cups with oil to ensure easy removal. Fill muffin cups almost full. Bake for 30 minutes.

Makes 18 muffins.

Variations: Sprinkle with turbinado sugar before baking, or for Cranberry Muffins, omit blueberries and add ½ cup chopped walnuts, 1 cup fresh, sliced cranberries, and 1 teaspoon grated orange zest.

Zucchini Muffins

When it comes to a rich source of potassium, zucchini takes the cake. One medium zucchini contains as much potassium as a medium banana, about 450 milligrams.

Ingredients

1 cup crushed pineapple, with juice
½ cup light olive oil
¾ cup Sucanat or turbinado sugar
½ cup soymilk
2 teaspoons vanilla
1 teaspoon salt
½ teaspoon stevia powder*
2 cups grated zucchini
1 cup chopped dates
1 cup walnuts, chopped
2½ cups whole wheat pastry four
2½ tablespoons Ener-G baking powder (or 1 tablespoon Rumford baking powder)
½ teaspoon coriander
scant ¼ teaspoon cardamom

Per muffin:
 Calories 225
 Protein 4 g
 Carbohydrates 31 g
 Fiber 3.5 g
 Fat 11 g
 Sodium 215 mg

Steps

1 Preheat oven to 350°.

2 Mix first seven ingredients in a large mixing bowl.

3 Grate zucchini and squeeze out juice. Add zucchini, chopped dates, and walnuts to bowl and mix.

4 Combine flour, baking powder, coriander, and cardamom in a separate bowl. Stir with a whisk to mix.

5 Fold flour mixture into wet ingredients, mixing well. Form muffins in oil-sprayed muffin tin with ice cream scoop.

6 Bake 40 to 45 minutes until lightly browned.

*The ½ teaspoon stevia powder may be substituted with 3 tablespoons more Sucanat or turbinado sugar.

Makes 18 muffins.

COOK'S TIP

This recipe may also be made as a cake, loaf, or mini-muffins with cooking time adjusted. Substitute carrots for zucchini for *Carrot Muffins.*

Cranberry Oat Muffins

Freeze some cranberries when they are available and you won't have to wait until the holidays to serve these muffins. Dense but delicious!

Ingredients

1 cup drained, crushed pineapple
1 ripe banana, mashed
¼ cup almond butter
¼ cup honey
½ teaspoon salt
1 teaspoon coriander
2 cups quick oats
¼ cup chopped walnuts
½ cup unsweetened coconut
1 cup date pieces
1 cup halved, fresh cranberries

Per muffin:
  Calories 260
  Protein 4 g
  Carbohydrates 35 g
  Fiber 5 g
  Fat 12.5 g
  Sodium 130 mg

Steps

1 Preheat oven to 350°.

2 Mix together pineapple, banana, almond butter, and honey in a large bowl.

3 Add remaining ingredients and mix well.

4 Spoon into oil-sprayed muffin tin. Heap mixture into the shape of a muffin, as they do not rise.

5 Bake for 45 minutes.

Makes 1 dozen muffins.

Banana Nut Bread

A breakfast bread that is perfect for a tea or brunch, it bakes to a beautiful golden brown.

Ingredients

½ cup light olive oil
2 teaspoons vanilla extract
1 cup frozen white grape juice concentrate
1¼ cups water
3 medium ripe bananas, mashed
1 cup unbleached flour
2 cups whole wheat pastry flour
⅓ cups date sugar
1½ teaspoons stevia powder
1 teaspoon salt
2½ tablespoons Ener-G baking powder or 1 tablespoon Rumford baking powder
¾ cup walnut pieces, coarsely chopped

Per slice:
    Calories 235
    Protein 3.5 g
    Carbohydrates 39.5 g
    Fiber 2 g
    Fat 7.5 g
    Sodium 150 mg

Steps

1 Preheat oven to 350°.

2 Mix wet ingredients in a bowl. Beat with a whisk for 100 strokes or 1 minute with an electric mixer.

3 Add bananas and walnuts to wet ingredients.

4 Mix dry ingredients in a separate bowl. Add liquid mixture and mix quickly and well. Pour into two oil-sprayed loaf pan and place directly into the oven.

5 Bake for 45 minutes.

Makes 16 slices or 18 muffins.

COOK'S TIP

Also makes very nice muffins, which need to bake only 30 to 35 minutes.

Orange Cranberry Bread

Fruity and festive, this recipe is a colorful addition to holiday fare.

Ingredients

20-ounce can crushed pineapple
1 tablespoon orange zest
¾ cup orange sections and juice
¼ cup frozen orange or pineapple
 juice concentrate
¼ cup honey
¼ cup tahini or light olive oil
1 cup cranberries
2 cups whole wheat flour
1 cup unbleached white flour
2 tablespoons Ener-G baking
 powder or 1 tablespoon
 Rumford baking powder
½ teaspoon salt
¼ cup golden raisins
½ cup chopped walnuts

Per slice:
 Calories 120
 Protein 2.5 g
 Carbohydrates 28 g
 Fiber 2.5 g
 Fat 3 g
 Sodium 45 mg

*"My Father giveth you the
true bread from heaven."*
 —John 6:32

Steps

1 Preheat oven to 375°. Drain some juice from the pineapple so that 1½ cups of pineapple and juice remain.

2 Blend the first six ingredients in a blender until smooth. The orange rind can be in little chunks since the mixture will be blended. Add the cranberries and pulse the blender briefly to chop.

3 Combine flours, baking powder, and salt in a large bowl and mix well. Fold blended mixture into dry ingredients, being careful not to stir out bubbles. Add the walnuts and raisins and stir briefly.

4 Bake in 3 small oil-sprayed loaf pans, approximately 3¼ x 5¾ inches in size, for 50 minutes. After 10 minutes, reduce oven temperature to 350°.

Makes 3 small loaves.

Pita Chips

Chips don't get any healthier than this! Serve with savory dips and enjoy the toasty flavor and great crunch. Use to dip into a thick Strawberry Smoothie, page 212, and the taste and texture experience is like an ice cream cone!

Ingredients

1 package whole wheat pita bread

Per 8 Pita Chips:
  Calories 30
  Protein 1.5 g
  Carbohydrates 7.5 g
  Fiber 1.4 g
  Fat .2 g
  Sodium 53 mg

Steps

1 Slice each pita loaf into eight triangles with a knife, or cut with scissors. Separate to single thickness.

2 Pile wedges onto a cookie sheet and bake at 125° overnight. These may also be baked one layer at a time at 300° for 15 to 20 minutes or until slightly browned.

3 Store in an airtight container.

Makes 12 servings.

HEALTH TIP

Another nutrient on which our bodies thrive is oxygen. Several times a day, take three or four slow, deep breaths. Oxygenation of the blood and the release of carbon dioxide will give you an energy boost if you're feeling sluggish.

Spreads & Dips

Guacamole recipe on page 78

66   Spreads & Dips

Tahini Garlic Butter

No blender is needed for this tasty, nutritious butter. Spread a generous layer on whole-grain bread slices and top with Sesame Sprinkle, page 93. Place it under the broiler until it begins to brown for an outstanding garlic toast.

Ingredients

⅓ cup tahini
½ teaspoon salt, scant
3 tablespoons water
¼ teaspoon garlic powder
    or 1 small clove garlic, pressed

Per 1 tablespoon:
    Calories 60
    Protein 1.5 g
    Carbohydrate 2 g
    Fiber .5 g
    Fat 4.5 g
    Sodium 150 mg

Steps

1 Whip ingredients together in a small bowl with a fork.

2 Keeps well in refrigerator for 10 days.

Makes ½ cup.

Apricot Preserves

A simple way to make a good thing better.

Ingredients

1 jar Apricot Polaner All Fruit
    Spreadable Fruit
¾ cup dried apricots, cut into
    ½-inch pieces

Per 2 tablespoons:
    Calories 70
    Protein .5 g
    Carbohydrates 17 g
    Fiber .5 g
    Fat 0 g
    Sodium 5 mg

Steps

1 Empty spreadable fruit into mixing bowl.
Add chopped apricots and stir to mix.

2 Store in refrigerator.

Makes 1 ½ cups.

Creamy Lemon Dip

A simple fruit platter can be made very special with this yummy dip. In the StepFast Lifestyle Series, an introduction to tofu is made via this recipe and the response is always, "I can't believe this is tofu!"

Ingredients

12.3 ounces firm, silken tofu
3 tablespoons lemon juice
½ teaspoon lemon extract
⅓ cup + 1 tablespoon pineapple
    juice concentrate
2 tablespoons water
1/16 teaspoon salt
1 tablespoon light olive oil

Steps

1 Place all ingredients into blender and blend until smooth.

2 Chill and serve with fresh fruit.

Makes 1¼ cups.

Per 2 tablespoons:
    Calories 50
    Protein 3 g
    Carbohydrates 4 g
    Fiber .5 g
    Fat 2.5 g
    Sodium 10 mg

Sunflower Sour Cream

Although this is somewhat different from sour cream, it makes a good accompaniment to baked potatoes and steamed vegetables. It's also an excellent raw vegetable dip.

Ingredients

½ cup raw sunflower seeds
½ cup hot, cooked brown rice
¾ cup water
¼ teaspoon dill weed
1 teaspoon salt
1½ teaspoons onion powder
½ teaspoon garlic powder
⅓ cup lemon juice

Per 2 tablespoons:
 Calories 40
 Protein 1.5 g
 Carbohydrates 3 g
 Fiber .5 g
 Fat 2.3 g
 Sodium 160 mg

Steps

1 Combine all ingredients in a blender and blend until smooth.

2 Place in refrigerator to chill.

Makes 2 cups.

Hummus

Originating in the Middle East, this delicious spread transcends almost all cultures and can be used in a variety of ways. One of my favorite things to do with hummus is to put it in a wrap along with lettuce, tomatoes, cukes, and olive slices. The sodium content is fairly high but evens out if served with lots of raw veggies. Also, the salt may be decreased if desired.

Ingredients

15.5-ounce can garbanzos, drained
1½ tablespoons lemon juice
2 tablespoons tahini or olive oil
½ teaspoon garlic powder
   or 1 clove fresh garlic
½ teaspoon salt (scant)
⅔ cup water
1 teaspoon cumin (optional)

Per ½ cup:
   Calories 215
   Protein 5 g
   Carbohydrates 22.5 g
   Fiber 6.5 g
   Fat 10 g
   Sodium 465 mg

Steps

1 Blend all ingredients until smooth. Home cooked garbanzos may be used, adjusting salt to taste according to the salt in garbanzos.

2 Serve with pita bread or *Pita Chips,* page 65, with raw veggies or use as sandwich or wrap filling.

Makes 1½ cups.

Jack Cheese Spread

A delicious, cheesy spread—sans fromage—that's "without cheese" in French! Great on sandwiches or with crackers. Makes a great grilled-cheese sandwich!

Ingredients

2 cups hot cornmeal mush*
¼ cup tahini
1½ teaspoons salt
¼ cup nutritional yeast flakes
1 tablespoon onion powder
¼ teaspoon garlic powder
1 tablespoon lemon juice

*To make cornmeal mush, bring 4 cups water to a boil in a medium saucepan. Gradually whisk in 1 cup of cornmeal. Stirring constantly, bring to a boil then reduce heat to simmer, cover and cook for 30 minutes. This may be used as a breakfast "side of grits," or as a hot cereal.

Per ¼ cup:
    Calories 75
    Protein 2.5 g
    Carbohydrates 10 g
    Fiber 1.5 g
    Fat 3.5 g
    Sodium 415 mg

Steps

1 In blender, whiz all ingredients until smooth. You may need to add another ¼-⅓ cup water, depending on how mushy the cornmeal mush is.

2 Pour mixture into a small serving bowl. Cool well and refrigerate until firm and spreadable.

Makes 14 servings.

COOK'S TIP

For *Jack Cheese Sauce,* add ½ cup water. Adjust the salt to taste.

Quick & Easy Cheese

More like a dip, this non-dairy cheese is perfect on a taco salad, burritos, or Pita Pizza, *page 146. The pimientos may be omitted for a substitute mozzarella on pizza or* Veggie Patch Flatbread, *page 122.*

Ingredients

12.3 ounces firm, silken tofu
2½ tablespoons tahini
    or sesame seeds
½ cup pimientos
½ cup water
2 tablespoons nutritional
    yeast flakes
2 tablespoons lemon juice
¾ teaspoon salt
1¼ teaspoons onion powder
¼ teaspoon garlic powder

Per 3 tablespoons:
    Calories 55
    Protein 4.5 g
    Carbohydrates 2.5 g
    Fiber 1.5 g
    Fat 3.5 g
    Sodium 125 mg

Steps

1 Combine all ingredients in a blender and blend until smooth.

2 Serve immediately or chill before serving.

Makes 15 servings.

COOK'S TIP

Substitute fresh red bell pepper for the pimiento for a wonderful flavor and to boost the amount of vitamin C. Also, 1½ cups of cooked millet or cornmeal mush may be substituted for tofu.

Tofu Mayonnaise

Most mayonnaise is quite high in fat because of the high oil content. This one is not only egg-free, but oil-free as well. It's also quite tasty and great for salad recipes.

Ingredients

⅓ cup raw sunflower seeds
    or rinsed raw, cashews
⅓ cup water
12.3 ounces firm, silken tofu
2½ tablespoons lemon juice
¾ teaspoon salt
½ teaspoon garlic powder
1 teaspoon onion powder

Per 2 tablespoons:
    Calories 45
    Protein 4 g
    Carbohydrates 1.5 g
    Fiber 1 g
    Fat 3 g
    Sodium 100 mg

Steps

1 Combine all ingredients in a blender and blend until smooth. A spatula may be used to stir during the blending process, but carefully!

2 Chill to thicken.

3 Keeps for 7–10 days in refrigerator.

Makes 1¼ cups.

Onion Dill Dip

The perfect addition to any party or picnic menu. Again, they won't believe it's tofu!

Ingredients

1 recipe of *Tofu Mayonnaise,* page 74
1 tablespoon lemon juice
1¼ teaspoons dill weed
1½ teaspoons onion powder
Salt to taste

Per 2 tablespoons:
    Calories 45
    Protein 4 g
    Carbohydrates 2 g
    Fiber 1 g
    Fat 3 g
    Sodium 100 mg

Steps

1 Combine all ingredients in a bowl and stir to mix.

2 Serve with chips (Baked Lays, baked tortilla chips, or *Pita Chips,* page 65) or raw veggies.

Makes 2¼ cups.

Minced Tofu Spread

Use this spread with additional Tofu Mayonnaise, *page 74, to make sandwiches and you will get rave reviews. With crusts removed and sandwiches quartered, you have perfect tea sandwiches for a reception.*

Ingredients

14 ounces firm, fresh tofu
½ cup minced onion
⅔ cup whole grain bread crumbs
⅓ cup parsley
½ cup pecans or walnuts
¼ cup Bragg Liquid Aminos
2 tablespoons peanut butter
½ teaspoon garlic powder
½ cup *Tofu Mayonnaise*

Per ⅓ cup:

    Calories 125
    Protein 9 g
    Carbohydrates 6 g
    Fiber 2 g
    Fat 8.5 g
    Sodium 410 mg

Steps

1 Mash tofu with a potato masher in a large bowl.

2 Mince onion in a small food processor. Add parsley and continue processing.

3 Add nuts and continue processing until all three ingredients are very fine.

4 Make bread crumbs separately in the food processor, by grinding whole grain bread.

5 In a large bowl, combine all ingredients with the tofu and mix well.

Makes 12 servings.

COOK'S TIP

Commercial breadcrumbs can be used, but homemade breadcrumbs are easily made by grinding *Whole Wheat Bread,* page 57, in a food processor and adding garlic powder and a sprinkle of Italian seasonings.

Hot Broccoli Dip

Especially around the holidays, this dip is very well received. It can be made ahead and reheated, adding the toasted almonds just before it goes on the table.

Ingredients

4 cups fresh chopped broccoli
　　or 10-ounce package frozen
　　chopped broccoli
1 medium onion, chopped
4-ounce can sliced or chopped
　　mushrooms, drained
1–2 cloves garlic, freshly pressed
½ cup sliced toasted almonds

Sauce ingredients:

1⅓ cups water
¼ cup raw, rinsed cashews
1½ tablespoons tahini
2 teaspoons lemon juice
1 teaspoon salt
2 tablespoons nutritional
　　yeast flakes
1½ teaspoons onion powder
½ teaspoon garlic powder
1 tablespoon cornstarch

Per ⅓ cup:
　　Calories 120
　　Protein 5 g
　　Carbohydrates 10 g
　　Fiber 4.5 g
　　Fat 8 g
　　Sodium 205 mg

Steps

1 Cook the broccoli while the sauce is being prepared. If using fresh, steam the broccoli with the chopped onion using a small steamer or in a small amount of water.

2 If using frozen broccoli, it may be cooked in the box in the microwave for 6 minutes, or follow directions on the box for stove-top preparation. Press any liquid out of the broccoli.

To make the sauce:

1 Blend the sauce ingredients in blender until smooth. Heat in large saucepan over medium-high heat until thickened.

2 Add broccoli, onion, mushrooms, and garlic and heat just until bubbly.

3 Add toasted almonds just before serving so they remain crisp.

4 Serve hot with dipping corn chips.

Makes 12 servings.

Guacamole

No fiesta is complete without guacamole!

Ingredients

2 ripe avocados (about 2 cups)
1 tablespoon chopped onion, or to taste
¼ teaspoon garlic powder or 1 small garlic clove, pressed
1 tablespoon lemon juice
½ teaspoon salt
⅓ cup finely diced tomato

Per ¼ cup:
    Calories 75
    Protein 1 g
    Carbohydrates 4.5 g
    Fiber 3 g
    Fat 6 g
    Sodium 120 mg

Steps

1 Mash avocados with a fork, or whiz in a small food processor.

2 Add remaining ingredients and stir to mix.

Makes 2½ cups.

COOK'S TIP

If not serving the guacamole immediately, cover with 1 teaspoon lemon juice to maintain green color. Pour off lemon juice and stir before serving.

Fresh Avocado Salsa

Garden fresh cherry tomatoes and just-pulled corn makes this salsa absolutely magnificent.

Ingredients

2 avocados, diced
2 ears raw corn, cut off cob
1 pint grape or cherry tomatoes, quartered
1 can black beans
juice of 1-2 limes, to taste
3 tablespoons fresh cilantro, chopped
¼ teaspoon salt or to taste

Per ½ cup:
    Calories 90
    Protein 3.5 g
    Carbohydrates 14 g
    Fiber 4.5 g
    Fat 4 g
    Sodium 160 mg

Steps

1 Pour black beans into colander and rinse.

2 Combine all ingredients in medium bowl and toss mix.

3 Serve with tortilla chips. Baked! Tostitos Scoops! are ideal to serve with this salsa.

Makes 6 cups.

Salsa

The world seems to be divided into two groups of people: those who love cilantro and those who don't. Both aromatic and therapeutic, cilantro is a key herb in many cuisines and central to salsa, though those who do not care for it can omit it! The lemon juice gives this a wonderful, fresh taste, and this recipe is almost as simple as opening a jar.

Ingredients

1 ½ cups chopped tomatoes (fresh or canned)
1 tablespoon lemon juice
1 ½ teaspoons cumin or to taste
½ teaspoon paprika
2 teaspoons onion, chopped small
¼ teaspoon salt
1 small clove of garlic, pressed
1 ½ teaspoons sweet basil
1 tablespoon chopped cilantro

Per ¼ cup:
    Calories 20
    Protein 1 g
    Carbohydrates 4 g
    Fiber 1 g
    Fat .5 g
    Sodium 150 mg

HEALTH TIP

Avoid heavy or late suppers and you will wake up with a sunny disposition!

Steps

1 Combine all ingredients in a blender, then pulse briefly, leaving vegetables chunky.

2 Taste and adjust salt, as it will vary according to the tomatoes used.

Makes 2 cups.

Seven-Layer Mexican Dip

A perfect dish to make for a festive gathering.

Ingredients

2 cups or 2 cans pinto beans, drained
½ cup diced tomatoes, drained
2 teaspoons *"No Alarm" Chili Powder,* page 25
1 clove pressed garlic
½ teaspoon dried oregano
1 recipe *Guacamole,* page 78
12.3 ounces firm, silken tofu
2 tablespoons lemon juice
½ teaspoon salt
½ teaspoon onion powder
2 medium vine-ripened tomatoes, diced
3 green onions, thinly sliced
½ cup sliced black olives

Per ½ cup:
    Calories 115
    Protein 6 g
    Carbohydrates 10 g
    Fiber 4 g
    Fat 6.5 g
    Sodium 360 mg

Steps

1 Blend pinto beans and diced tomatoes, chili powder, garlic, and oregano in a blender until chunky.

2 Spread into 9 x 13-inch casserole dish.

3 Prepare *Guacamole* according to recipe. Spread over bean mixture.

4 Blend tofu, lemon juice, salt, and onion powder in the blender until smooth. Spread tofu mixture over guacamole.

5 Top with diced tomatoes, sliced onions, and sliced black olives.

6 Chill for at least 1 hour. Serve with tortilla chips.

Makes 15 servings.

Salads &
Salad Dressings

Southwestern Salad recipe on page 92

Apple Walnut Salad for Two

Commonly known as Waldorf salad, this original recipe was created not by the chef, but by the maître d'hôtel of New York's Waldorf-Astoria in 1896.

Ingredients

½ cup Vegenaise
1 teaspoon honey
1 large apple (Braeburn, Red, or
    Golden Delicious)
2 tablespoons walnuts, coarsely
    chopped
1½ tablespoons raisins

Per ½ recipe:
    Calories 210
    Protein 6.5 g
    Carbohydrates 28.5 g
    Fiber 4 g
    Fat 10 g
    Sodium 225 mg

Steps

1 Combine Vegenaise and honey in a mixing bowl. (*Tofu Mayonnaise*, page 74, may also be used, but the higher fat version works better.)

2 Core and dice apple and add to mayonnaise mixture along with walnuts and raisins.

3 Mix well and chill before serving.

Makes 2 servings.

HEALTH TIP

A medium-sized apple contains about 80 calories and is a good source of potassium and fiber. The fiber in apples is a mix of soluble and insoluble fiber, safeguarding against heart disease and colon cancer at the same time.

Fruit Salad

If you are trying to lower your sodium intake, eat more fruit. And to keep it interesting, make some creative fruit salads. Around the holiday season, a beautiful and festive combination is fresh pineapple, apples, grapes, star fruit, and pomegranate seeds. They look like jewels!

Ingredients

20-ounce can pineapple chunks or tidbits in juice
1 large apple, cored and diced
1 banana, sliced
1 cup sliced strawberries or blueberries

Per 1 cup without variations:
    Calories 110
    Protein 1 g
    Carbohydrates 28.5 g
    Fiber 3.5 g
    Fat .3 g
    Sodium 2 mg

Steps

1 Mix and serve. Other fruits of your choice (cherries, kiwi, grapes, orange sections, pears, peaches, and melons in season).

2 For a heartier salad, chopped nuts, coconut, raisins, dates, or other chopped dried fruit can be added.

Makes 5 servings.

COOK'S TIP

Golden Delicious, Gala, and Braeburn apples are consistently crisp and sweet and provide a wonderful texture to this salad.

Spinach Salad

Bags of prewashed spinach make this salad convenient to make, and it's a welcomed change from conventional tossed salad.

Ingredients

½ cup slivered almonds
2 quarts fresh spinach
¼ cup grated carrots
¼ cup lemon juice
½ teaspoon dried basil leaves
⅛ teaspoon thyme
2 tablespoons sesame seeds
⅛ teaspoon onion salt
2 cloves garlic, pressed

Per serving:
    Calories 150
    Protein 6 g
    Carbohydrates 9 g
    Fiber 4 g
    Fat 12 g
    Sodium 65 mg

Steps

1 Toast almonds at 300° for 10 minutes or until lightly toasted. Watch almonds closely to prevent burning. Set aside.

2 Carefully wash and tear spinach into bite-sized pieces. Add carrots.

3 Combine remaining ingredients and shake in a jar to make a dressing.

4 Toss spinach, carrots, and almonds with dressing just before serving.

Makes 6 servings.

Beets & Baby Greens Salad

After you've tasted fresh beets, you will never go back to eating canned or bottled beets. And after trying them raw, you may never bother to cook them again!

Ingredients

1 medium fresh beet
4 cups of baby salad greens
¼ cup chopped onion of your
    choice, sliced
½ cup coarsely chopped walnuts

Per 1½ cup:
    Calories 125
    Protein 4 g
    Carbohydrates 8 g
    Fiber 3 g
    Fat 9.5 g
    Sodium 30 mg

Steps

1 Peel and grate beet on coarse side of grater.

2 Toss greens, onions, and cucumber together and create a bed of greens on salad plates. Top with grated beets and walnuts.

3 Serve with *Ruby Raspberry Dressing,* page 87.

Makes 4 servings.

Ruby Raspberry Dressing

Beautiful and full of flavor, this dressing packs a great nutritional punch too.

Ingredients

½ cup white grape raspberry juice
    concentrate
½ cup lemon juice
¼ cup flax seed oil
¼ cup olive oil
1 teaspoon Vegesal or salt
2 teaspoons Instant Clear Jel

Per 2 tablespoons:
    Calories 95
    Protein .1 g
    Carbohydrates 5.5 g
    Fiber .1 g
    Fat 8.5 g
    Sodium 390 mg

Steps

1 Place all ingredients except the Instant Clear Jel in a blender.

2 Blend well and sprinkle Instant Clear Jel into dressing while blender is running on medium speed.

3 Chill and serve over any fresh, tossed salad.

Makes 1 ½ cups.

"I have often wondered why people take better care of their cars than their bodies. I have yet to meet a person who said, 'God has a plan as to when my car should die, and I do not need to worry about it.'"

—Neil Nedley, M.D.

Dill Dressing

Fresh onion, garlic and lemon juice give this dressing a real punch. Fresh dill makes it even better.

Ingredients

1 cup rinsed, raw cashews
1 cup water
⅓ cup lemon juice
¾ teaspoon salt
1½ teaspoons onion powder or
    1½ tablespoons fresh onion
½ teaspoon garlic powder or
    1 clove garlic
½ teaspoon dried dill weed or
    1 tablespoon fresh dill

Per 2 tablespoons:
    Calories 75
    Protein 2.5 g
    Carbohydrates 4 g
    Fiber .5 g
    Fat 6 g
    Sodium 100 mg

Steps

1 Blend all ingredients until smooth.

2 Chill and serve.

Makes 2¼ cups.

Italian Dressing

A very versatile dressing, this Italian Dressing *keeps in the refrigerator for 10 to 14 days.*

Ingredients

¼ cup lemon juice
¼ cup olive oil
½ cup water
1 tablespoon honey
2 teaspoons chicken-style seasoning
½ teaspoons salt
1 large clove garlic
½ teaspoon Italian seasonings
1 teaspoon parsley
2 teaspoons Instant Clear Jel

Per 2 tablespoons:
  Calories 55
  Protein .1 g
  Carbohydrates 2.5 g
  Fiber 0 g
  Fat 5 g
  Sodium 205 mg

Steps

1 Blend all ingredients except Instant Clear Jel in blender until smooth.

2 Sprinkle in Instant Clear Jel while blending.

3 This dressing will thicken further as it chills.

Makes 1⅓ cups.

Toasted Sesame Dressing

The Vine Restaurant in Benton, Tennessee, has a marvelous menu of scrumptious vegan items. The salads offer a beautiful array of color and texture, and some are dressed with this delightful Toasted Sesame Dressing.

Ingredients

¼ cup raw, rinsed cashews
⅓ cup nutritional yeast flakes
⅓ cup lemon juice
½ cup water
½ cup toasted sesame oil
½ cup olive oil
1 teaspoon onion powder
1 teaspoon ground marjoram
2 teaspoons salt
2½ tablespoons honey
2 cloves fresh garlic

Per 2 tablespoons:
    Calories 125
    Protein 1.5 g
    Carbohydrates 5 g
    Fiber 1 g
    Fat 11.5 g
    Sodium 260 mg

Steps

1 Blend all ingredients in blender until smooth. Keeps in refrigerator for about 2 weeks.

Makes 2 cups.

COOK'S TIP

This dressing is excellent drizzled inside a tortilla wrap, filled with hummus, sliced tomatoes, cukes, lettuce, and olives.

Ranch Dressing

Fresh lemon juice is best when it comes to salad dressings, especially this one.

Ingredients

¼ cup raw sunflower seeds
¼ cup tahini
3 tablespoons fresh onion in chunks
¾ teaspoon salt
¾ cup water
4 tablespoons lemon juice
1 large clove garlic
½ teaspoon dill weed
2 teaspoons parsley flakes

Per 2 tablespoons:
    Calories 35
    Protein 1 g
    Carbohydrates 2 g
    Fiber .5 g
    Fat 3 g
    Sodium 140 mg

Steps

1 Combine all ingredients except dill weed and parsley flakes in a blender and blend until smooth.

2 Add herbs and blend again for about 5 seconds.

Makes 1⅔ cups.

Southwestern Salad

Many restaurants serve a similar salad and include chunks of chicken breast. SoyCurls prepared with chicken-style seasoning will add taste and texture to this salad, though it's quite good as is.

Ingredients

6 cups romaine lettuce, torn
1 avocado, diced
16-ounce can black beans, drained
1 cup corn, canned, fresh or frozen
2 cups diced tomatoes, canned
    or fresh
1 cucumber, diced
½ cup red onion, chopped
1 recipe *Mexi-Texi Ranch Dressing*
½ cup fresh cilantro, chopped

Per salad:
    Calories 375
    Protein 16.5 g
    Carbohydrates 56 g
    Fiber 19.6 g
    Fat 13 g
    Sodium 625 mg

Steps

1 Place 1½ cups of the lettuce on individual plates. Top each salad with ⅓ cup *Mexi-Texi Ranch Dressing* (see recipe below).

2 Layer with black beans, avocado, corn, tomatoes, cucumber, and red onion. Sprinkle each salad with 2 tablespoons of cilantro.

3 Serve with corn chips.

Makes 4 large salads.

For Mexi-Texi Ranch Dressing

Combine 1 cup *Salsa*, page 80, and 1 cup *Ranch Dressing*, page 91, in a bowl and mix well.

Makes 2 cups.

Sesame Sprinkle

A dry dressing for salad or cooked veggies, this is a great take-along idea for work or travel. Sesame seeds are an excellent source of calcium, and this recipe contains 270 mg. per serving.

Ingredients

1 cup hulled sesame seeds
¼ cup nutritional yeast flakes
1 teaspoon onion powder
½ teaspoon garlic powder
½ teaspoon salt

Per 2 tablespoons:
    Calories 140
    Protein 5 g
    Carbohydrates 7.5 g
    Fiber 4.2 g
    Fat 11 g
    Sodium 120 mg

Steps

1 Place all ingredients into a dry blender or ½ recipe at a time into an electric coffee mill.

2 Mill until seeds are ground and ingredients are well combined.

3 Serve with lemon juice over salad, baked potato, or steamed vegetables; use for garlic bread or as a parmesan cheese substitute. Freezes well.

Makes 10 servings.

"Better by far to have less expensive clothing and furniture, than to scrimp the supply of necessary articles for the table."
—Ellen G. White

Soy Curls Salad

Wow! Stuff a tomato, make a sandwich, or fill mini-pastry shells for a magnificent summertime treat!

Ingredients

1 cup dry Soy Curls
2½ cups water
1 tablespoon chicken-style
    seasoning
½ cup diced celery
¾ cup *Tofu Mayonnaise*, page 74,
    or Vegenaise
¼ cup pickle relish
2 teaspoons chicken-style seasoning
    (or to taste)

Per ½ cup:
    Calories 90
    Protein 6 g
    Carbohydrates 8.5 g
    Fiber 2 g
    Fat 4 g
    Sodium 100 mg

Steps

1 Hydrate Soy Curls for 1 hour or overnight in water and 1 tablespoon chicken-style seasoning. This process can be sped up by bringing broth and Soy Curls to a boil in a saucepan. Then remove from heat and allow to cool.

2 Drain Soy Curls well in colander or large strainer. Squeezing liquid out with your hand works even better. This should be 1½ cups re-hydrated Soy Curls.

3 Place in food processor and grind into small pieces. This can be done more simply with a knife.

4 Combine with the remaining ingredients.

5 Chill and use just like chicken salad. Delicious served in pita bread with tomato slices and sprouts.

Makes 6 servings.

"So I am living without fats, without meat, without fish, but am feeling quite well this way. It always seems to me that man was not born to be a carnivore."

—Albert Einstein

Tofu Egg Salad

Superior in taste and nutrition, this vegan version is easier to prepare than a conventional egg salad. Perfect in a pita and a nice tea sandwich filling.

Ingredients

14 ounces fresh, firm tofu
½ cup finely chopped celery
¾ cup Vegenaise
    or *Tofu Mayonnaise,* page 74
¼ cup sweet lemon pickle relish
¾ teaspoon turmeric
1 teaspoon onion powder
½ teaspoon garlic powder
2 teaspoons chicken-style seasoning
Salt to taste

Per ½ cup:
    Calories 90
    Protein 6 g
    Carbohydrates 8.5 g
    Fiber 1.5 g
    Fat 4 g
    Sodium 100 mg

Steps

1 Mash tofu until fine in medium bowl.

2 Add remaining ingredients and mix well.

Makes 4 servings.

Tomato Basil Salad

The time to make this salad is when the tomatoes come in fresh from the garden. I like to peel the tomatoes so they are perfectly tender. Outstanding with Gazpacho, *page 101, and* Honey Wheat Bread, *page 55, with avocado slices on a warm summer day.*

Ingredients

3 vine-ripened tomatoes
½ small red onion, thinly sliced
15-ounce can white beans, drained
¼ cup fresh basil leaves, chopped
3 tablespoons lemon juice
1 tablespoon olive oil
½ teaspoon salt

Steps

1 Slice tomatoes into ½-inch wedges, cutting again if tomatoes are large. Place into a medium-sized bowl.

2 Combine with onion and beans that have been drained and rinsed.

3 Add basil, lemon juice, olive oil, and salt and toss to mix. Chill slightly and allow flavors to blend.

Makes 4 servings.

Per 1 cup:
Calories 165
Protein 9 g
Carbohydrates 28.5 g
Fiber 6.5 g
Fat 3 g
Sodium 300 mg

COOK'S TIP

If fresh basil is not available, use 1½ teaspoons of dried basil. It is still delicious!

Kale Salad

Colorful and calcium-rich, this salad keeps well in the refrigerator for several days, and the raw kale is surprisingly tender.

Ingredients

⅓ cup fresh lemon juice
3 tablespoons Bragg Liquid Aminos
⅓ cup water
½ teaspoon garlic powder or
    1 large clove, pressed
1 teaspoon onion powder
7 cups fresh, raw kale, finely
    chopped
4 scallions, chopped
½ sliced ripe olives
⅓ cup raw sunflower seeds
½ cup red bell pepper, diced

Per 1 cup:
    Calories 150
    Protein 6.5 g
    Carbohydrates 12 g
    Fiber 4 g
    Fat 10.5 g
    Sodium 480 mg

Steps

1 Combine first 5 ingredients in a jar and shake to make the dressing.

2 Toss kale, olives, and scallions in a large bowl. Pour the dressing over the salad and stir to mix. Allow to marinate about an hour or overnight.

3 Just before serving, add the sunflower seeds and red bell pepper.

Makes 8 cups.

Greek Salad

Another garden-to-table recipe, this salad is delicious with or without the tofu.

Ingredients

½ pound tofu, extra firm
2 tablespoons chicken-style
    seasoning
2 cups water
2½ cups tomatoes, diced
3 cups cucumbers, peeled and
    diced
½ cup red onion, chopped
½ teaspoon garlic powder or 1
    clove, pressed
¼ cup lemon juice
2 tablespoon olive oil (optional)
1 teaspoon salt
½ teaspoon oregano leaves
¼ cup fresh basil, chopped (or 2
    teaspoons dried)
1 cup pitted whole black olives

Steps

1 Dice tofu into ¾ inch cubes. Boil tofu for 15 minutes in the 2 cups water with the chicken-style seasoning added. Drain and cool.

2 Combine with remaining ingredients and toss.

3 Chill and allow flavors to blend.

Makes 8 servings.

Per ½ cup serving, without olive oil:
    Calories 60
    Protein 3.5 g
    Carbohydrates 5.5 g
    Fiber 1.5 g
    Fat 3 g
    Sodium 540 mg

Dilled Cucumbers

Summer's bounty from the garden usually includes lots of cucumbers and this is a refreshing way to serve them. Sliced sweet onion or chopped spring onion tops may be added as well.

Ingredients

1 large cucumber
3 tablespoons lemon juice
¼ teaspoon salt
1 teaspoon dill weed
¼ cup water

Per ⅙ recipe:
    Calories 10
    Protein .5 g
    Carbohydrates 2.5 g
    Fiber .5 g
    Fat 0 g
    Sodium 60 mg

Cook's Tip

If in a hurry, place several ice cubes on the cukes to chill.

Steps

1 Peel cucumber in a striped fashion and slice into rounds.

2 Toss with remaining ingredients. Salt to taste. Much of the salt will remain in the lemon water.

3 Chill and serve.

Makes 6 servings.

"Daniel's clearness of mind and firmness of purpose, his strength of intellect in acquiring knowledge, were due in a great degree to the plainness of his diet, in connection with his life of prayer."

—Ellen G. White

Soups & Stews

Cuban Black Bean Soup recipe on page 108

Ultimate Gazpacho

Gazpacho is a traditional Spanish soup, served cold, that you can make as chunky as you like. Raw and robust, the flavor and nutrition are absolutely bursting out of this soup.

Ingredients

4 cups tomatoes
1 cup cucumber
2 tablespoons olive oil
⅓ cup lemon juice
½ teaspoon salt
1 medium garlic clove
½ cup red bell pepper, finely diced
¼ cup onion, chopped
½ cup cilantro or parsley, chopped

Per 1¼ cup:
    Calories 70
    Protein 2 g
    Carbohydrates 10 g
    Fiber 2 g
    Fat 3.5 g
    Sodium 205 mg

Steps

1 Pulse in a blender 2 cups of the tomatoes and the cup of cucumber, olive oil, lemon juice, salt, and garlic. Pour into a large bowl. This mixture should be thick and slightly chunky.

2 All the remaining vegetables, including the remaining tomatoes, should be chopped or diced very fine.

3 Mix the chopped vegetables with the ingredients that have been blended.

4 Serve cold on a hot summer day, or any time!

Makes 6 servings.

French Onion Soup

Again, we thank the French for another classic recipe. Minus the cheese, this version is still delicious and somewhat lower in sodium. Perfect for supper fare on a chilly evening.

Ingredients

3 medium onions, thinly sliced
1 tablespoon olive oil
8 cups water
3 tablespoons chicken-style seasoning
½ cup Bragg Liquid Aminos
2 tablespoons onion powder
1 tablespoon maple syrup

Per 1¼ cup:
    Calories 45
    Protein 2.5 g
    Carbohydrates 9 g
    Fiber 1 g
    Fat 1 g
    Sodium 850 mg

Steps

1 Sauté onions in a large pot in the olive oil until slightly browned.

2 Add water and seasonings and allow to simmer for 20 minutes.

3 For a real treat, top each cup of soup with a few croutons, then top with a slice of soy cheese. Place the bowl in the microwave on high for about 30 seconds to melt the cheese.

Makes 8 servings.

Soy Curls Noodle Soup

This vegan version works just as well as the often-prescribed chicken noodle soup for those feeling a little under the weather—in fact, it's probably better!

Ingredients

1 tablespoon minced garlic
½ cup chopped onion
6 cups water
2 cups dry whole grain pasta,
   ribbon style if available
1 cup Soy Curls
1½ tablespoons chicken-style
   seasoning
1 teaspoon dried parsley
   or 2 tablespoons finely chopped
   fresh parsley

Per 1 cup:
   Calories 300
   Protein 13.5 g
   Carbohydrates 20 g
   Fiber 1 g
   Fat 2 g
   Sodium 150 mg

Steps

1 In a large pot, lightly steam onion and garlic in ½ cup of the water.

2 Place remaining water, pasta, and chicken-style seasonings into a pot and bring it to a boil. Add remaining ingredients and bring to a boil. Allow to boil gently for 8 to 10 minutes.

3 Add Soy Curls and parsley, and cook on medium heat until pasta is tender. Salt to taste.

Makes 6 servings.

COOK'S TIP

A nice addition to this soup is a handful of thoroughly washed fresh spinach. Add it to the soup and continue cooking another 3 minutes. If Soy Curls are unavailable, cooked garbanzos can be used.

Corn Chowder

Slightly sweet, this chowder can be made with fresh, frozen, or a good-quality canned corn. An excellent choice to serve with a fruit meal that includes muffins and fruit salad.

Ingredients

¾ cup rinsed, raw cashews
2½ cups water
1 tablespoon cornstarch
1 teaspoon onion powder
1 teaspoon salt*
½ teaspoon honey or turbinado
    sugar
2 cups cooked corn

*Adjust salt according to the amount of salt in the corn that is used.

Per 1¼ cup:
    Calories 340
    Protein 10.5 g
    Carbohydrates 35 g
    Fiber 4.5 g
    Fat 21 g
    Sodium 590 mg

Steps

1 Place all ingredients except 1 cup of the corn in a blender and blend until smooth.

2 Pour mixture into a saucepan and cook on medium heat until thickened.

3 Add the remaining cup of corn and stir to heat thoroughly. Serve hot.

Makes 4 servings.

COOK'S TIP

Soymilk could be substituted for the cashews and water. Even a sweetened variety would work well. You will need 3 cups.

Broccoli Soup

Tahini and nutritional yeast flakes provide a cheesy flavor without any dairy products in this flavorful cream soup. Try cauliflower, asparagus, or celery instead of broccoli.

Ingredients

5½ cups unsweetened soymilk
  or nut milk
3 cups, fresh broccoli, chopped
2 tablespoons nutritional yeast
  flakes
½ teaspoon garlic powder
  or 1 clove pressed
½ cup chopped, steamed onions
1 teaspoon salt
1 tablespoon tahini
¼ cup cornstarch
¼ teaspoon turmeric

Per 1 cup:
   Calories 130
   Protein 8.5 g
   Carbohydrates 16.5 g
   Fiber 3.2 g
   Fat 4.5 g
   Sodium 320 mg

HEALTH TIP

Another excellent source of potassium, one cup of broccoli contains 460 mg.

Steps

1 Heat 5 cups milk, nutritional yeast flakes, garlic powder, tahini, salt and turmeric in a medium saucepan, but do not boil.

2 Place broccoli and onions in steamer and steam until tender.

3 Mix cornstarch with remaining ½ cups milk. Add to heated milk and cook on low heat, stirring constantly until thickened.

4 Add steamed broccoli and onion to thickened soup. Serve hot.

Makes 8 servings.

Butternut Squash Soup

Rich in beta carotene, potassium, and other minerals, butternut squash is one of the most delicious winter squashes. They are easy to grow, so be sure to plant some in your garden and look forward to serving this satisfying soup on a chilly winter day.

Ingredients

1 medium butternut squash
2 medium apples
1 medium onion
4 cups water
1 teaspoon salt
13.5-ounce can coconut milk
dash of cayenne (optional)

Per 1 cup:
    Calories 155
    Protein 2 g
    Carbohydrates 19 g
    Fiber 3 g
    Fat 9 g
    Sodium 300 mg

Steps

1 Peel butternut squash and cut into large chunks. You will need about 6 cups. Cut apples and onion into large chunks.

2 Combine the squash, apples, and onion in a large pot with the water. Cook until tender.

3 Puree cooked ingredients in blender. Pour back into pot. Add salt, coconut milk, and cayenne if desired and stir until blended.

4 Bring to a boil and serve hot.

Makes 8 cups.

Cajun Gumbo des Herbes

"Des herbes" means vegetable gumbo. Even the "chicken" in this version is a vegetable!

Ingredients

2 tablespoons olive oil
2 tablespoons flour
6 cups water
1 tablespoon chicken-style
   seasoning
1 cup dry Soy Curls or 2 cups
   seasoned tofu
1 bunch scallions, with tops
¾ cup fresh parsley, chopped fine
½ cup green pepper, diced
1 15-ounce can diced tomatoes
2 bay leaves
1 dash cayenne
½ teaspoon salt or to taste
1 cup fresh or frozen okra, sliced
2 cups cooked brown rice

Per 1 cup:
   Calories 160
   Protein 8 g
   Carbohydrates 18 g
   Fiber 2.5 g
   Fat 7 g
   Sodium 750 mg

Steps

1 Combine olive oil and flour to make a roux in a heavy-bottom soup pot. Brown this mixture on medium-high heat, stirring constantly, until the color of peanut butter.

2 Stir in water and bouillon and bring to a boil.

3 Add remaining ingredients, except okra and rice, and allow to return to a boil. Simmer on low about 15 minutes

4 Add okra and cook an additional 10 minutes.

5 Serve in bowls with a scoop of brown rice.

Makes 8 cups.

Cuban Black Bean Soup

Soup and salad with a whole grain bread make a complete meal when you serve a hearty bean soup like this one.

Ingredients

1 pound dry black beans
7 cups water
1 onion, chopped
2 cloves fresh garlic, pressed
2 stalks celery
1 teaspoon olive oil
    or 2 tablespoons water
½ teaspoon dried oregano
1 teaspoon cumin (optional)
15-ounce can stewed tomatoes
1 teaspoon salt

Per 1¼ cup:
    Calories 215
    Protein 12.5 g
    Carbohydrates 39 g
    Fiber 9 g
    Fat 1.5 g
    Sodium 400 mg

Steps

1 Sort and rinse black beans and cook with water overnight on low in a crockpot. Remove liquid to achieve desired consistency.

2 In a skillet, sauté in oil or steam onion, garlic, and celery until soft. Add oregano and cumin if desired.

3 Add the sautéed mixture, salt, and the tomatoes to the crockpot. Continue to cook for 30 minutes.

Makes 8 servings.

Red Lentil Soup

India's protein-rich classic dish has many varieties, and this one is simple and savory. Variations can include the addition of different squashes.

Ingredients

1 medium onion, chopped
1 red bell pepper, diced
3 carrots, sliced
2 medium potato, diced
1 cup red lentils, rinsed
4 cups water
1 tablespoon chicken-style
　　seasoning
2 cloves garlic, minced
1 tablespoon mild curry powder
½ teaspoon salt or to taste
2 tablespoons olive oil

Per cup:
　　Calories 175
　　Protein 7.5 g
　　Carbohydrates 27 g
　　Fiber 4.5 g
　　Fat 4 g
　　Sodium 370 mg

Cook's Tip

See *Special Ingredients,* page 26, for mild Curry Powder recipe.

Steps

1 Steam onions and red pepper in a small amount of water in a heavy-bottom stock pot.

2 Add carrots, potatoes, lentils, and water. Bring to a boil, then cover and simmer for about an hour.

3 Add remaining ingredients and simmer a few minutes more.

4 Serve over brown rice or with whole wheat chapattis or pita bread.

Makes 8 servings.

Lentil Tomato Stew

We can thank Charlotte and Katrina (AKA "Charlie" and "Bean") for this tasty stew that's quick and hearty.

Ingredients

1 cup dry lentils
3 cups water
1 can diced tomatoes
1 medium onion, diced
3 cloves garlic, sliced
1 teaspoon dried basil
½ cup quick-cooking brown rice
½ teaspoon salt, or to taste

Per 1¼ cup:
Calories 270
Protein 16 g
Carbohydrates 51 g
Fiber 16.5 g
Fat 1 g
Sodium 360 mg

"Trust in the LORD, and do good; so shalt thou dwell in the land, and verily thou shalt be fed."

—*Psalm 37:3*

Steps

1 Bring lentils and water to a boil in a large saucepan. Turn to low heat and simmer for 30 minutes.

2 Add remaining ingredients and simmer an additional 15 to 20 minutes.

3 Add water if more "soup" is desired.

Makes 4 servings.

I love spending time in the kitchen with Charlotte, my daughter. She's a great cook!

Mom's Chili

This chili takes just 10 minutes to make, and it's good!

Ingredients

1 cup onion, chopped
1 cup green pepper, diced
1 cup vegeburger (optional)
26.5-ounce can non-chunky style spaghetti sauce
16-ounce can dark red kidney beans
14.5-ounce can diced tomatoes with juice
½ tablespoon *"No Alarm" Chili Powder,* page 25
½ cup water

Per 1¼ cup:
    Calories 200
    Protein 12.5 g
    Carbohydrates 30.5 g
    Fiber 10 g
    Fat 4 g
    Sodium 900 mg

Steps

1 Steam onion and green pepper in small amount of water in a large saucepan.

2 Add remaining ingredients and bring to a boil. Turn down and simmer for a few minutes.

3 Serve over *Baked Brown Rice,* page 159, over a baked potato, or in a bowl with *Whole Wheat Bread,* page 57, or crackers.

Makes 6 servings.

COOK'S TIP

See *Special Ingredients* on page 25 for *"No Alarm"* Chili Powder recipe.

Navy Bean Soup

For years I thought bean soup would lack flavor without what most people consider an essential ingredient: a ham bone. Yet herbs, vegetables, and salt in combination with these navy beans make an incredibly delicious soup, with no animal fat.

Ingredients

1 pound dry navy beans (2½ cups)
7 cups water
1 bay leaf
1 cup grated carrots
1 cup chopped celery
1 cup chopped onion
1 teaspoon chicken-style seasoning
½ teaspoon salt
1 teaspoon onion powder
½ teaspoon garlic powder
½ teaspoon ground marjoram
¼ teaspoon sage
¼ teaspoon thyme

Per 1 cup:
    Calories 195
    Protein 12 g
    Carbohydrates 35 g
    Fiber 14 g
    Fat 1 g
    Sodium 250 mg

Steps

1 Sort, wash, and cook beans in a crockpot on low overnight with the water and bay leaf.

2 Steam carrots, celery, and onion until tender.

3 Combine steamed veggies with beans and add remaining ingredients.

Makes 8 servings.

COOK'S TIP

Raw carrots, celery, and onions can be added to crockpot in the morning; then continue cooking for several hours.

Split Pea Soup

This high-fiber soup has almost no fat, yet it is flavorful and satisfying. Enjoy it any time of the year.

Ingredients

2 cups dry split peas
7½ cups water
1 large onion, chopped
1 bay leaf
1 large carrot, sliced
2 stalks celery, sliced
1 clove garlic, pressed (optional)
2 teaspoons salt

Per ¾ cup:
    Calories 170
    Protein 11.5 g
    Carbohydrates 32 g
    Fiber 6.5 g
    Fat 0.5 g
    Sodium 600 mg

"Research makes evident that foods high in fiber lead to a lower rise in blood sugar, and as a result, require less insulin to handle the meal."

—Neil Nedley, M.D.

Steps

1 Sort and wash split peas. Cook the peas, onion, and bay leaf with water in large sauce pan for about 45 minutes. Bring to a boil on high, then reduce heat and cover.

2 Add remaining ingredients and simmer ½ hour more or until vegetables are tender.

Makes 6 cups.

Ratatouille

Harvest time is the perfect time to prepare this vegetable stew. Add some black beans and you have a complete entrée.

Ingredients

1 large onion, chopped
1 green pepper, diced
1 clove fresh garlic, pressed
1 tablespoon olive oil
2 medium zucchini, diced
1 medium eggplant, diced
3 tomatoes, diced
½ cup water
1 teaspoon salt
½ teaspoon dried basil
¼ teaspoon dried oregano

Per 1¼ cup:
    Calories 60
    Protein 2.5 g
    Carbohydrates 12 g
    Fiber 4.5 g
    Fat 1.5 g
    Sodium 305 mg

Steps

1 Use a large, heavy-bottomed saucepan with a lid. Sauté the onion, garlic, and green pepper in olive oil while dicing the other vegetables.

2 Add zucchini, eggplant, and water and stir. Cover and steam for 5 minutes. Add tomatoes, cover and simmer for 30 minutes or until all vegetables are well cooked.

3 Uncover and turn up the heat to allow some of the liquid to evaporate. Serve over *Baked Brown Rice,* page 159.

Makes 8 servings.

"No occupation is so delightful to me as the culture of the earth, and no culture comparable to that of the garden."

—Thomas Jefferson

Vegetable Barley Soup

Quick and hearty!

Ingredients

1 small onion, chopped
1 clove fresh garlic, pressed
1 stalk celery, sliced
1 tablespoon olive oil or
    2 tablespoons water
1 carrot, diced
1 medium potato, diced
3 cups water
2 teaspoons chicken-style seasoning
14.5-ounce can whole tomatoes
¼ cup dry barley
½ cup garbanzo beans
1 teaspoon dried basil
1 teaspoon parsley flakes
1 cup okra, sliced

Per 1 cup:
    Calories 125
    Protein 3.5 g
    Carbohydrates 22 g
    Fiber 4.5 g
    Fat 3 g
    Sodium 300 mg

Steps

1 In a large saucepan, steam or sauté onion, garlic, and celery until tender.

2 Add all remaining ingredients except okra. Bring to a boil, cover and simmer for 10 minutes.

3 Add okra and continue cooking for 15 minutes, until okra is tender.

Makes 6 servings.

"Grains, fruits, nuts, and vegetables constitute the diet chosen for us by our Creator. They impart a strength, a power of endurance, and a vigor of intellect, that are not afforded by a more complex and stimulating diet."

—Ellen G. White

Entrées

Stuffed Mushrooms recipe on page 123

Entrées

Linguine with Artichoke Hearts

Sal's Bistro prepares a pasta entrée very similar to this one and provided the idea for this recipe.

Ingredients

8 ounces dry linguine
2 tablespoons olive oil
1 small onion, chopped
1 clove fresh garlic, pressed
6 large mushrooms
13.75-ounce can artichoke hearts
½ cup *Spaghetti Sauce,* page 172
½ teaspoon dried basil
½ teaspoon salt
1 medium vine-ripened tomato

Per serving:
    Calories 205
    Protein 7.5 g
    Carbohydrates 31 g
    Fiber 9.5 g
    Fat 8 g
    Sodium 600 mg

Steps

1 Bring 3 quarts of water to a boil. Cook linguine according to directions.

2 Sauté onion and garlic in ½ tablespoon of the olive oil for 3 minutes in a large skillet. Add mushrooms that have been stemmed and quartered into wedges and continue sautéing for 5 minutes.

3 Drain artichoke hearts and chop in half each way. Add artichokes, sauce, basil, and salt to the skillet. Stir, and continue to cook on low heat.

4 Dip tomato into the boiling water with the linguine for 15 seconds. Rinse with cold water and remove the skin. Slice into very thin wedges and add to the skillet. Cook only several minutes longer.

5 Drain the linguine when al dente (done "to the bite") and add to the skillet. Add the remaining 1½ tablespoons olive oil and toss.

Makes 4 servings.

Lasagna

Perfect for a potluck, as it can be made ahead of time and serves a crowd.

Ingredients

7 cups *Spaghetti Sauce,* page 172
1 recipe *Spinach Ricotta-Style Filling*
½ pound uncooked lasagna
    noodles
¾ cup soy cheese or *Quick & Easy
    Cheese,* page 73
½ cup water

Per 2 x 2-inch serving:
    Calories 154
    Protein 10.5 g
    Carbohydrates 19 g
    Fiber 5 g
    Fat 6 g
    Sodium 710 mg

Steps

1 Make layers in a 9 x 13-inch pan,
starting with a layer of *Spaghetti Sauce,*
then a layer of uncooked noodles, then a full
recipe of *Spinach Ricotta-Style Filling.* Top
with another layer of noodles, and sprinkle
the remaining sauce and the ½ cup water
evenly over the top.

2 Cover and refrigerate overnight.

3 Soy cheese or *Quick & Easy Cheese*
can be added just prior to baking, or
if serving later, top with cheese prior to
reheating. For best results, bake, allow to
cool and set, and reheat prior to serving.

4 Bake at 350° for 45 minutes.

Makes 12 servings.

COOK'S TIP

For gluten-free lasagna, slice
zucchini lengthwise into ¼-inch
flat strips for use in place of
the lasagna noodles. Place the
zucchini slices on an oil-sprayed
baking sheet and add a sprinkle
of salt and Italian seasonings.
Bake at 425° for 20 minutes,
turning over once halfway
through baking. Proceed with
lasagna recipe.

Variation: Add steamed
spinach, carrots, and/or
squash after layer of *Spinach
Ricotta-Style Filling.*

Spinach Ricotta-Style Filling

Lasagna, manicotti, and stuffed pasta shells are all scrumptious with this delicious tofu filling. Easy to prepare and rich in tryptophan and B vitamins, these Italian favorites are great make-ahead entrées.

Ingredients

14 ounces tofu, extra firm, mashed
1½ cups sautéed, chopped onion
10 ounces frozen chopped spinach
2 teaspoons garlic powder
2 teaspoons sweet basil
1 teaspoon salt
1 tablespoon honey
1 tablespoon lemon juice
2 tablespoons nutritional yeast
   flakes
½ teaspoon oregano

Steps

1 Cook spinach, using directions on box or by placing the whole box in the microwave for 6 minutes.

2 Combine spinach with remaining ingredients in large bowl and mix well.

3 Use for *Lasagna,* page 118, or for *Stuffed Shells* (see below).

Makes 8 servings.

Per ½ cup:
  Calories 105
  Protein 10.5 g
  Carbohydrates 9 g
  Fiber 3.5 g
  Fat 4.5 g
  Sodium 325 mg

COOK'S TIP

For *Stuffed Shells,* cook shells and fill with filling. Place in a casserole dish with the bottom covered with sauce. Spoon sauce across each shell but do not completely cover. Cover with foil, being careful not to touch shells. Bake 30 minutes at 350°.

Soy Curls Cacciatore

Soy Curls provide optimum nutrition, as well as taste and texture and incredible versatility. This is just one more traditional chicken recipe that works exceptionally well with Soy Curls. Presents well with brown rice or pasta.

Ingredients

1½ cups water with ½ teaspoon salt
1 cup Soy Curls
1 cup onion, diced
2 stalks celery, diced
2 teaspoons olive oil (optional)
28-ounce can diced tomatoes
2 teaspoons chicken-style seasoning
1 clove garlic, pressed

Per 1 cup:
    Calories 130
    Protein 5.5 g
    Carbohydrates 20 g
    Fiber 4.7 g
    Fat 4 g
    Sodium 940 mg

Steps

1 Rehydrate Soy Curls in the salt water for 30 minutes.

2 In a non-stick skillet, sauté onion, garlic, and celery in olive oil or steam in small amount of water until tender.

3 Pour water off Soy Curls and add them to the mixture.

4 Add tomatoes and chicken-style seasoning* and simmer for 5 minutes.

5 Serve over *Baked Brown Rice,* page 159.

* If chicken-style seasoning is not available, simply add ¼ teaspoon garlic powder, 1½ teaspoons onion powder, and ¼-½ teaspoon Italian seasonings.

Makes 4 servings.

"Daniel purposed in his heart that he would not defile himself with... the king's delicacies, nor with the wine which he drank..."

—Daniel 1:8

Italian Eggplant

Serve with a side of whole-grain blend spaghetti, more sauce, and a salad for an Italian meal that's simple and delicious.

Ingredients

1 large eggplant
4 cups *Spaghetti Sauce,* page 172
¾ cup *Sesame Sprinkle,* page 93

Per ⅛ recipe:
    Calories 160
    Protein 5.5 g
    Carbohydrates 16 g
    Fiber 7 g
    Fat 9.5 g
    Sodium 445 mg

Steps

1 Wash and slice eggplant into 3/8-inch slices. Sprinkle bottom of 2 casserole dishes with *Sesame Sprinkle.*

2 Arrange eggplant, single layer, in both casserole dishes. Lightly cover with *Sesame Sprinkle.*

3 Cover with *Spaghetti Sauce* and bake at 350° for 45 minutes.

4 Remove from oven, sprinkle with *Sesame Sprinkle* again, and serve.

Makes 8 servings.

Veggie Patch Flatbread

As colorful and appealing as it is delicious, this casual fare is always very well received.

Ingredients

2 12-inch whole wheat flatbread or
    pita bread loaves
1 tablespoon olive oil or water
1 medium zucchini
1 medium onion
2 cloves fresh garlic, sliced
½ of a red or green bell pepper
¼ teaspoon salt
3.5-ounce can sliced ripe olives
½ teaspoon Italian seasoning
2 small tomatoes
1 recipe *Quick & Easy Cheese,*
    page 73

Per slice:
    Calories 180
    Protein 8.5 g
    Carbohydrates 25 g
    Fiber 4.5 g
    Fat 7 g
    Sodium 670 mg

Steps

1 Sauté or steam zucchini, onions, and pepper in oil or water for 5 minutes

2 Spread flatbread with *Quick & Easy Cheese* from which the pimiento has been omitted.

3 Arrange sliced tomatoes and sautéed vegetables on top of cheese, top with sliced olives, and sprinkle with Italian seasoning.

4 Bake at 350° for 15 minutes using a pizza pan.

Makes 8 slices.

"Worship the LORD your God, and his blessing will be on your food and water. I will take away sickness from among you... I will give you a full life span."

—Exodus 23:25, 26 (NIV)

Stuffed Mushrooms

Studies have revealed that some mushroom varieties have significant antioxidant qualities, the shiitake and mitake mushrooms in particular. In fact, history tells us that Chinese emperors consumed Shiitake mushrooms in large quantities to fend off old age. Portabella mushrooms are growing in popularity as well, but this recipe uses large white mushrooms, though others could be substituted. Served as an appetizer or entrée, stuffed mushrooms are a pleasant change from ordinary fare.

Ingredients

1 pound medium-sized mushrooms
1 tablespoon olive oil
1 celery stalk, diced small
3½ ounces firm tofu, diced
1 medium zucchini, diced small*
1 medium carrot, diced small
1½ cups stuffing mix
2 tablespoons chopped fresh basil,
    or 1 teaspoon dried basil
⅔ cup of water

Glaze:
½ cup + 1 tablespoon water
1 teaspoon Bragg Liquid Aminos
2 teaspoons cornstarch
¼ teaspoon onion powder
¼ teaspoon garlic powder

*Chopped broccoli stems may
  be substituted.

Per 2 mushrooms:
    Calories 170
    Protein 7 g
    Carbohydrates 25 g
    Fiber 2.5 g
    Fat 4.5 g
    Sodium 550 mg

Steps

1 Remove the stems from the mushrooms and chop fine. Reserve the caps.

2 Heat the olive oil in a large, heavy-bottomed skillet over a medium heat. Add the chopped mushroom stems, celery, tofu, zucchini, and carrot and cook for 3 to 4 minutes, stirring occasionally.

3 While vegetables are steaming, combine all glaze ingredients in a small saucepan and whisk to mix thoroughly. Cook glaze over medium-high until thickened. Set aside.

4 Stir the bread crumbs and chopped basil into the vegetable mixture. Add salt to taste and mix thoroughly.

5 Spoon the mixture into the mushroom caps. Pour the glaze into a shallow ovenproof dish and tilt to coat the bottom. Place the mushrooms in the dish on top of the glaze.

6 Bake in preheated oven at 425° for 20 minutes, or until cooked through.

Makes 8 servings.

Pictured on page 116

Shish Kabobs

This cooking method and presentation gives a superb taste and appeal to simple food. Great make-ahead summer fare.

Ingredients

1 red or green bell pepper
1 small onion
12 cherry tomatoes
14 ounces fresh, extra firm tofu
1 recipe *Italian Marinade,* page 173

Per shish kabob:
    Calories 190
    Protein 6.5 g
    Carbohydrates 13 g
    Fiber 2 g
    Fat 14 g
    Sodium 260 mg

Steps

1 Dice tofu into 1-inch pieces. Slice pepper, zucchini, and onion into 1-inch pieces.

2 Place the tofu and all the vegetables in a bowl with the marinade and allow them to marinate for 30 minutes.

3 Make the shish kabobs, alternating the veggies and tofu. Place on a pre-heated grill or under the broiler for approximately 8 minutes. Rotate skewers and cook the other side for 5 to 8 minutes.

4 Serve with brown or wild rice.

Makes 6 servings.

"The LORD God planted a garden... and out of the ground the LORD God made every tree grow that is pleasant to the sight and good for food."

—*Genesis 2:8, 9*

Holiday Loaf

Though it resembles stuffing, this recipe is too good to be served on the side! With Baked Tofu, *page 131, gravy, and traditional Thanksgiving fare, this loaf can easily play center stage.*

Ingredients

2 cups whole grain bread cubes
2 cups cooked brown rice
½ cup chopped walnuts
1 green pepper, chopped
2 stalks celery, diced
¼ cup rinsed, raw cashews
1 cup water
1 cup minced onion
2 tablespoons Bragg Liquid Aminos
½ teaspoon salt
1 tablespoon parsley flakes
1 teaspoon sage

Per ¾ cup:
    Calories 270
    Protein 9.5 g
    Carbohydrates 38 g
    Fiber 6 g
    Fat 11 g
    Sodium 690 mg

COOK'S TIP

A serving suggestion is to alternate *Baked Tofu,* page 131, slices with scoops of *Holiday Loaf* in a casserole dish. Bake as above and serve with *Herb Gravy,* page 169.

Steps

1 Combine bread cubes, rice, walnuts, celery, pepper, and onion in a large bowl.

2 Blend cashews and water until smooth. Add to dry ingredients. Add seasoning and mix well.

3 Press into oiled loaf pans or small casserole dish. Bake covered 45 minutes at 350°. Bake uncovered for an additional 15 to 20 minutes.

4 If slicing is desired, allow to cool completely, slice, and arrange on ovenproof platter, then reheat 15 to 20 minutes at 300°.

Makes 8 servings.

Millet Loaf

A small, round, yellow grain, millet packs a powerful nutritional punch. With more protein, B vitamins, iron, and copper than whole wheat, it is also a rich source of phosphorus. Millet has a subtle, nut-like flavor and alkaline and gluten-free.

Ingredients

½ cup raw cashews
1 cup water
1 cup wheat germ or bread crumbs
1½ cups cooked millet
½ cup quick oats
1 medium onion, chopped
1 tablespoon chicken-style
    seasoning
½ teaspoon garlic powder
2 tablespoons Bragg Liquid Aminos
    or soy sauce
½ teaspoon sage

Per ⅛ loaf:
    Calories 165
    Protein 5.5 g
    Carbohydrates 20.5 g
    Fiber 2 g
    Fat 7.5 g
    Sodium 495 mg

Steps

1 Blend cashews and water until smooth.

2 Combine well with remaining ingredients in a mixing bowl.

3 Pack into oil-sprayed loaf pan or casserole dish. Bake at 350° for 25 to 30 minutes.

4 Patties can also be formed and browned in a non-stick skillet.

5 Serve with gravy for a formal meal, or this loaf makes an excellent sandwich filling with lettuce, tomato, and *Tofu Mayonnaise*, page 74.

Makes 8 servings.

COOK'S TIP

To prepare cooked millet, bring 3 cups of water and 1 cup of millet to a boil in a medium saucepan. Reduce heat to low, cover, and simmer for 30 minutes. Add a sprinkle of salt to serve as is for a breakfast cereal or use it in recipes. This will yield 3½ cups of cooked millet. It freezes well for future use.

Soy Curls & Rice

Served with a salad, Soy Curls & Rice *is a superb one-dish meal. Get creative and add whatever vegetables you have on hand.*

Ingredients

1 cup dry Soy Curls
2 cups water
1 teaspoon chicken-style seasoning
    or salt
½ cup chopped onion
¼ cup diced red pepper
¼ cup frozen peas
1½ cups cooked brown rice
1 teaspoon olive oil (optional)
1 tablespoon Bragg Liquid Aminos
½ teaspoon Vegesal or salt
    to taste
⅓ cup toasted slivered almonds

Per 1 cup:
    Calories 230
    Protein 9 g
    Carbohydrates 23 g
    Fiber 4.5 g
    Fat 12.5 g
    Sodium 750 mg

Steps

1 Place Soy Curls, water, and chicken-style seasoning in a saucepan. Bring to a boil. Simmer for 5 minutes. Pour off the broth. Chop Soy Curls to desired size.

2 Steam onion and red pepper in ¼ cup water for 5 minutes. Add frozen peas and steam 1 more minute. Add rice, olive oil, seasonings, and Soy Curls.

3 Toss to mix and top with almonds and serve.

Makes 4 servings.

HEALTH TIP

For a good night's sleep and to help maintain your ideal weight, eat a light evening meal several hours before bedtime or skip supper altogether. Make it a habit, and your stomach will stop talking back to you!

Soy Curls with Coconut Lime Sauce

A taste of the Caribbean right here at home!

Ingredients

1½ cups dry Soy Curls*
3 cups water
2 tablespoons chicken-style
    seasoning
1 medium onion, sliced
13.5-ounce can coconut milk
1 tablespoon cornstarch
2 tablespoons lime juice

*Strips of *Baked Tofu,* page 131,
  can substituted for the Soy Curls.

Per serving:
    Calories 300
    Protein 7.5 g
    Carbohydrates 14.6 g
    Fiber 4 g
    Fat 19 g
    Sodium 426 mg

Variations: Add steamed
slivers of green and red bell
pepper for a beautiful dish.
This recipe is also delicious
made with lemon juice instead
of lime juice.

Steps

1 Place Soy Curls, water, and 1 tablespoon of the chicken-style seasoning in a medium saucepan. Bring to a boil, then remove it from the heat.

2 In a skillet, steam the onion with a small amount of water until tender.

3 Drain the Soy Curls and add them to the skillet. Add the additional tablespoon of chicken-style seasoning and the coconut milk and bring the mixture to a boil.

4 Mix the cornstarch and the lime juice in a small bowl and add to the skillet, stirring until the sauce is thickened. It will thicken more as it cools.

5 Serve with *Baked Brown Rice,* page 159, and garnish with chopped scallions if desired.

Makes 4 servings.

Best Oat Burgers

Moist and delicious, these are the best I've tasted. With lettuce, tomato, and mayonnaise on a quality whole wheat bun, no one will be wondering where the beef went!

Ingredients

4½ cups water
¼ cup Bragg Liquid Aminos
3 tablespoons olive oil
4½ cups old-fashioned oats
1 cup pecan meal
2 teaspoons onion powder
½ teaspoon garlic powder
1 teaspoon salt
1 teaspoon basil

Per burger:
   Calories 190
   Protein 7 g
   Carbohydrates 24 g
   Fiber 4.5 g
   Fat 9 g
   Sodium 165 mg

Variation: For breakfast sausage, add 1½ teaspoon sage.

COOK'S TIP

Any leftover burgers can be frozen for later use. LaChoy Lite Soy Sauce may be substituted for the Bragg Liquid Aminos.

Steps

1 Bring water, Bragg Liquid Aminos, and olive oil to boil in a large saucepan.

2 Add oats and simmer for 10 minutes. Remove from heat. Add remaining ingredients and mix well.

3 Allow to cool just slightly and form into patties on oil-sprayed cookie sheet, using a round ¼-cup measure or ice cream scoop to make uniform patties. With wet fingers, flatten patties and round edges.

4 Bake at 350° for 30 to 35 minutes.

Makes 20 burgers.

Garden Burgers

The ingredients for burgers with this name could vary as much as do vegetables from the garden. This version is delicious, but you might want to experiment with whatever vegetables you have on hand.

Ingredients

½ cup finely chopped onion
½ cup grated carrots
⅓ cup chopped black olives
2 cups cooked brown rice
2 tablespoons flaxseed meal
1 tablespoon olive oil
2 tablespoons tomato purée
2 teaspoons nutritional yeast flakes
1 teaspoon onion powder
1 clove fresh garlic, pressed
2 teaspoons parsley flakes
1 teaspoon basil
¾ teaspoon salt

Per burger:
    Calories 90
    Protein 2 g
    Carbohydrates 13 g
    Fiber 2.2 g
    Fat 4 g
    Sodium 475 mg

Steps

1 Combine all ingredients in a bowl and mix well. Let stand just a few minutes to absorb liquid.

2 Form round flat patties on non-stick cookie sheet. Bake at 350° for 35 to 40 minutes or until beginning to brown on the bottom.

Makes 8 burgers.

COOK'S TIP

If short of time, simply press entire recipe into an oil-sprayed loaf pan, cover, and bake at 350° for 45 to 50 minutes. Remove cover for last 10 minutes. Cool slightly before slicing.

Baked Tofu

A great chicken substitute, this tofu recipe is extremely quick, very tasty, and can be served as an entrée or used in other recipes. Serve with stuffing and gravy for an excellent holiday entrée.

Ingredients

14 ounces fresh, firm tofu
1 tablespoon chicken-style
   seasoning
¾ cup water
2 tablespoons Bragg Liquid Aminos
2 tablespoons nutritional yeast

Per 2 slices:
   Calories 125
   Protein 14 g
   Carbohydrates 5 g
   Fiber 3 g
   Fat 7 g
   Sodium 215 mg

Steps

1 Cut tofu into slices ¼-inch thick (10 slices).

2 Mix remaining ingredients in a bowl and sprinkle over tofu.

3 Bake uncovered at 350° for 30 to 40 minutes or until beginning to dry out a bit.

Makes 10 slices.

Shown here with Holiday Loaf, *page 125.*

Seasoned Tofu

Here's the simplest way to turn tofu into savory chunks of meat substitute. When seasoned, the tofu is ready to add to stir-fries, salads, soups, and sandwiches. Any tofu will work, and it will become firmer when chilled. Perfect for chicken-style salad.

Ingredients

14 ounces fresh, firm tofu
1 tablespoon Bragg Liquid Aminos

Per ⅕ recipe:
    Calories 115
    Protein 13 g
    Carbohydrates 3.5 g
    Fiber 2 g
    Fat 7 g
    Sodium 145 mg

Steps

1 Break up tofu into bite-sized pieces into a non-stick skillet. Sprinkle with Bragg Liquid Aminos. Cook, stirring often, over medium heat until firm and beginning to brown.

2 Use in *Vegetable Stir Fry,* page 134, or in any other recipe in which you would use with chunks of chicken.

Makes 5 servings.

French Lentils

Varying in color and variety, lentils are packed with protein and rich in other nutrients. French lentils are smaller than other lentils, cook quickly, and hold their shape well. They are particularly nice served on a plate rather than as a stew.

Ingredients

2 cups dry French lentils
4 cups water
½ cup finely chopped onion
1 teaspoon salt

Per ½ cup:
Calories 95
Protein 7 g
Carbohydrates 17 g
Fiber 6.6 g
Fat .3 g
Sodium 237 mg

Steps

1 Bring lentils, water, and onion to a boil. Reduce heat to medium-low and continue to cook for 30 minutes, until almost dry.

2 Serve with *Polenta,* page 158, and *Picadillo Sauce,* page 177.

Makes 10 servings.

"The beef industry has contributed to more American deaths than all the wars of this country, all natural disasters, and all automobile accidents combined. If beef is your idea of "real food for real people," you'd better live real close to a real good hospital."

—Neal Barnard, M.D., President, Physicians' Committee for Responsible Medicine

Vegetable Stir Fry

Tofu or Soy Curls make great additions to the veggies you choose to include in this Asian favorite. Keep some Baked Brown Rice, *page 159, on hand in the freezer to quickly thaw and heat for a complete meal.*

Ingredients

2 medium carrots, sliced
2 stalks celery, sliced
1 red bell pepper, cut into strips
1 medium onion, cut into strips
1 can sliced water chestnuts
2 cups broccoli florets or asparagus
½ cup toasted slivered almonds
1 cup *Oriental Glaze,* page 175

Per 1 serving:
    Calories 165
    Protein 5.5 g
    Carbohydrates 17 g
    Fiber 5.5 g
    Fat 10 g
    Sodium 215 mg

COOK'S TIP

For additional protein, add seasoned tofu or Soy Curls.

Steps

1 Steam carrots and celery for 5 minutes in large skillet with lid in ½ cup water. Add onions and continue steaming for 3 minutes.

2 Add broccoli and red bell pepper and steam an additional 3 minutes.

3 Add drained water chestnuts and toasted almonds.

4 Pour off any remaining water. Add *Oriental Glaze* and serve over brown rice. See *Baked Brown Rice.*

Makes 6 servings.

Sweet & Sour Soy Curls

Preparation of this tasty dish is quick and easy as no pre-hydrating is necessary. In a matter of minutes, dinner will be on the table!

Ingredients

1 tablespoon olive oil or water
1 onion, chopped
1 bell pepper, sliced in 1-inch slices
4½ cups Soy Curls
3½ cups water
2 tablespoons Bragg Liquid Aminos
    or soy sauce
1½ tablespoons brown sugar or
    Sucanat
½ teaspoon salt
1 tablespoon lemon juice
2 tablespoons nutritional yeast
    flakes

Per serving:
    Calories 135
    Protein 11.5 g
    Carbohydrates 10 g
    Fiber 4.5 g
    Fat 6.5 g
    Sodium 315 mg

Steps

1 Steam or sauté onion and pepper in a large skillet until tender.

2 Add Soy Curls and water and bring to a boil. Reduce heat, cover, and simmer for 5 minutes.

3 Add seasonings and stir well. Simmer an additional 5 minutes, stirring occasionally.

4 Serve immediately over *Baked Brown Rice,* page 159.

Makes 8 servings.

HEALTH TIP

Meat, cheese, and all other animal products are completely devoid of fiber, a vital nutrient that plays a critical role in controlling weight and blood sugar, as well as in preventing colon cancer.

Crockpot Beans

Using the crockpot to cook beans is the absolute simplest way to prepare them. Split peas and lentils cook quickly and are best cooked on top of the stove; I use the crockpot for all other legumes. Add a little seasoning and serve them as they are or incorporate them into your favorite recipes.

Ingredients

3 cups dry beans
9 cups water
1–2 teaspoons salt, to taste
2 teaspoons onion powder
½ teaspoon garlic powder

Per ½ cup:
Calories 118
Protein 8 g
Carbohydrates 21 g
Fiber 5 g
Fat .5 g
Sodium 300 mg

Steps

1 Sort beans on a dry dish towel, removing shriveled or discolored beans, as well as any foreign matter (rocks, etc.).

2 Wash beans in colander and place in a crockpot with water. Cook on low overnight or on high for 5 hours.

3 Add salt and other seasonings after beans are cooked.

Makes 8 cups.

"The doctor of the future will give no medicine, but instead will interest his patients in the care of the human frame, in diet, and in the cause and prevention of disease."

—Thomas Edison

Burrito Beans

The old-fashioned "soak and cook" method is used here, but for convenience sake, I prefer the crockpot method (see page 136). You can even use canned beans to prepare refried beans for burritos, without frying them even the first time!

Ingredients

1 pound pinto or pink beans
1 medium onion, diced
1 teaspoon olive oil (optional)
1½ teaspoons salt

Per ½ cup:
    Calories 115
    Protein 7 g
    Carbohydrates 19.5 g
    Fiber 5 g
    Fat 1.4 g
    Sodium 250 mg

Steps

1 Sort the beans, then soak them overnight in a large kettle with plenty of water.

2 In the morning, pour the water off and use fresh water, about 10 cups, to cook the beans until tender, about 2½ hours. You might also use the crockpot method.

3 Purée the beans in a blender with a little water. Add raw onion to the beans in the blender, or you might want to sauté the onion in water or olive oil and then add the blended beans to the skillet.

4 Add salt to taste. Serve with heated tortillas, diced tomatoes, shredded lettuce, chopped onions, olives, and brown rice.

Makes 7 cups.

COOK'S TIP

To bake and serve, fill tortillas with the bean mixture, diced tomatoes, rice, and soy cheese, then roll and place in a casserole dish. Cover with *Picadillo Sauce*, page 177, and bake at 350° for 20 minutes.

Pastelon Asteca

This Spanish dish translates into Mexican lasagna, a perfect one-dish meal. Pinto or black beans can be cooked in large quantities in the crockpot and divided to use in this and other recipes.

Ingredients

1 recipe of *Burrito Beans,* page 137, or use Taco Bell canned refried beans
14 6-inch corn tortillas
1 cup sliced black olives
14 ounces shredded soy cheese or *Healthy Melty Cheese,* page 171
2 cups *Picadillo Sauce,* page 177

Per serving:
  Calories 160
  Protein 8 g
  Carbohydrates 22 g
  Fiber 5 g
  Fat 5 g
  Sodium 475 mg

Steps

1 Arrange the ingredients in a casserole dish, as with lasagna: sauce, corn tortillas, some sauce, and beans. Arrange two layers and on the top layer add sauce, soy cheese or *Healthy Melty Cheese,* and sliced black olives.

2 Warm in 350° oven for about 30 minutes, until bubbly.

Makes 12 servings.

HEALTH TIP

Eating high-fiber foods causes a sense of fullness sooner than low-fiber foods, which signals the brain to stop eating before we overeat. Pass the whole wheat bread, please!

Zucchini Stacks

The perfect recipe for those zucchini that grow to a foot long overnight! Don't choose the extremely large ones as the seeds might be tough. Three inches in diameter at the largest point is just right, and these stacked veggies are just delicious.

Ingredients

1 medium onion, diced
⅓ package of Gimme Lean
    mock sausage
1 teaspoon each oregano,
    coriander, and cumin
1 28-ounce can whole, peeled plum
    tomatoes, drained; or 3 cups
    peeled, fresh tomatoes wedges
1 tablespoon olive oil
1 large zucchini
2 tablespoons chopped, fresh
    parsley or basil

Per stack:
    Calories 117
    Protein 8 g
    Carbohydrates 15 g
    Fiber 3.5 g
    Fat 4 g
    Sodium 380 mg

Steps

1 Steam onion in small amount of water in large skillet.

2 As it is steaming, add mock sausage and break up into pieces with spatula. Cook until the onion is tender.

3 Add seasoning, oil, and tomatoes, breaking up tomatoes somewhat. If using fresh tomatoes, salt to taste.

4 Slice zucchini into ⅜-inch slices. Arrange the four largest ones on the bottom of an 8 x 8-inch baking dish.

5 Spoon the sauce over each slice, top with the next slices, add more sauce and continue with smaller slices and more sauce, three layers high.

6 Top stacks with chopped parsley or basil.

7 Bake for 30 to 40 minutes at 375°. Serve with pasta and additional sauce.

Makes 4 servings.

Kids' Stuff

Alphabet Soup recipe on page 145

Fruity Oatmeal

Choose your favorite fruit to add to the hot oatmeal. Fruity bursts of flavor provide a change of pace from this traditional favorite. Adding a banana makes it taste like warm banana pudding!

Ingredients

1 cup old-fashioned oats
¼ teaspoon salt
1¾ cups water
1 banana, peach, pear or berries

Per 1¼ cup:
  Calories 355
  Protein 13.8 g
  Carbohydrates 65.5 g
  Fiber 9.8 g
  Fat 5.6 g
  Sodium 297 mg

Steps

1 Prepare oatmeal by bringing water and salt to a boil. Add oats and stir. Cover and reduce heat to low and simmer for 20 minutes.

2 Prepare fruit by chopping or slicing it into small chunks.

3 Just before serving, add sliced fruit, stir, and keep on low heat for one minute.

4 Serve with soymilk and top with nuts or granola if desired.

Makes 2 servings.

COOK'S TIP

If using apples or pears, add during last 10 minutes so the fruit cooks somewhat. Berries, mango, papaya, and banana may be added at the end.

"Dr. Benjamin Spock, perhaps the most influential pediatrician of all time, says children should stick to a vegetarian diet, devoid of all dairy products after the age of 2. That advice is contained in the seventh edition of his world-famous book, Baby and Child Care, *issued in May, 1998."*

—Jane E. Brody

Jungle Gems

Kids love this treat from the tropics!

Ingredients

1 medium mango, peeled and cubed
1 small papaya, peeled and cubed
1 banana, sliced
1½ cups fresh pineapple chunks
¼ cup unsweetened shredded coconut
¼ cup toasted slivered almonds

Per ½ cup:
    Calories 120
    Protein 2 g
    Carbohydrates 16 g
    Fiber 3 g
    Fat 6.5 g
    Sodium 5 mg

Steps

1 Toss fruit and coconut just before serving.

2 Top with toasted almonds and serve.

Makes 5 cups.

HEALTH TIP

Mangos are rich in beta-carotene, vitamins C and E, and soluble fiber. Fresh mangoes are firm but soft to the touch and are best from May to September.

Pineapple Breakfast Pudding

It was an adult who reminded me to include this recipe, but the kids love it!

Ingredients

1 cup fresh pineapple chunks
⅓ cup almonds
1 fresh pear, cored and quartered
12.3 ounces firm, silken tofu
¼ cup pitted dates
¼ teaspoon salt

Per ½ cup:
  Calories 130
  Protein 6 g
  Carbohydrates 16 g
  Fiber 3g
  Fat 6 g
  Sodium 120 mg

Steps

1 Blend all ingredients until smooth.

2 Serve with granola or Grapenuts, and fresh fruit.

Makes 6 servings.

French Toast House

This cozy cottage puts a smile on the little ones' faces every time.

Ingredients

2 pieces of *French Toast,* page 46

Per house:
- Calories 320
- Protein 10.5
- Carbohydrates 39.5 g
- Fiber 5.5 g
- Fat 15.5 g
- Sodium 425 mg

Steps

1 Follow the recipe for *French Toast* made with cashews or the *Quick French Toast,* page 47. Brown slowly so *French Toast* is firm. Two slices of *French Toast* will be needed for each house.

2 Cut off the crust of both pieces and reserve. Cut a door in one piece, but leave it in place.

3 Take the other piece and cut diagonally in half, creating two triangles. Place one triangle on the top of the house to make a roof.

4 Cut a piece of crust 1½ inches long with a diagonal cut on one end; it fits on the roof to make a chimney.

5 Cut the crust into ½-inch pieces and place them like flagstones leading up to the door.

6 The one who makes the *French Toast House* gets to eat the leftover scraps, and they are yummy!

Makes 1 house.

Alphabet Soup

The kids will spell "Thank you" when they find this fun soup in their bowl. Make it quickly with frozen or canned vegetables.

Ingredients

1 small onion, chopped
1 stalk celery, sliced
1 can whole tomatoes
1 medium potato, diced
1 carrot, diced
3 cups water
2 teaspoons chicken-style seasoning
½ cup corn
½ cup peas
¼ cup whole wheat alphabet
    noodles

Per 1 cup:
    Calories 75
    Protein 2.5 g
    Carbohydrates 16.5 g
    Fiber 3 g
    Fat .5 g
    Sodium 275 mg

Steps

1 Steam onion and celery in a small amount of water or sauté in olive oil.

2 Add tomatoes, potatoes, carrots, water, and chicken-style seasoning. Bring to a boil and simmer for 15 minutes

3 Add corn, peas, and alphabet noodles and continue cooking for 10 minutes.

Makes 8 servings.

Pita Pizza

Plan a pizza bar and let everyone make their own so they can "have it their way." Throw the leftover fixings into the salad and you've got a party!

Ingredients

1 package whole wheat pita bread
Spaghetti Sauce, page 172,
 or pizza sauce
Quick & Easy Cheese, page 73

Topping ideas: Diced tomatoes,
 chopped onions, garlic, peppers,
 sliced black olives, *Best Oat
 Burger* crumbles, zucchini,
 yellow squash

Per pizza:
 Calories 260
 Protein 13 g
 Carbohydrates 37 g
 Fiber 8.5 g
 Fat 9.5 g
 Sodium 1135 mg

Steps

1 Spread sauce on pita bread. Top with
 toppings of your choice.

2 Spoon cheese on top. *Healthy Melty
 Cheese* or a commercial soy mozzarella
can be used.

3 Sprinkle with Italian seasonings and
 finish with sliced black olives.

4 Bake at 400° directly on oven rack for
 10 minutes. Serve immediately.

Makes 8 servings.

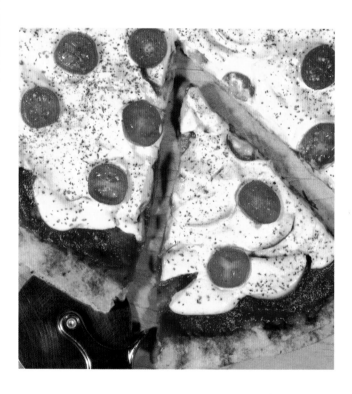

*"Oh, give thanks to the
LORD, for He is good! For
His mercy endures forever."*

—Psalm 107:1

Beans 'n Franks

Hot dogs, links, franks … by any name, the kids love them, and so does everyone else!

Ingredients

1 medium onion
1 clove fresh garlic, pressed
1 teaspoon olive oil
3 cups cooked beans
4 vegetarian hot dogs
1 tablespoon molasses
4 tablespoons tomato purée
Salt to taste

Per 1 cup:
Calories 210
Protein 14 g
Carbohydrates 24 g
Fiber 7 g
Fat 6.5 g
Sodium 530 mg

Steps

1 Sauté onion and garlic in olive oil, or steam in a small amount of water, for about 5 minutes in a large saucepan.

2 Cut the vegetarian hot dogs into ½-inch pieces.

3 A combination of beans can be used, including pinto, kidney, and cannelloni beans. Canned or home-cooked will work. Include some of the liquid in either case, and combine the beans with the onions, garlic, franks, and remaining Ingredients.

4 Pour into a casserole dish, cover, and bake at 350° for 1 hour. For a quicker version, simply heat in the saucepan until bubbly.

Makes 6 servings.

Zucchini Patties

Nobody said they're crab cakes, but with a little tartar sauce, I begin to hear the waves lapping. Well, okay, you try it!

Ingredients

1 cup *Tofu Mayonnaise*, page 74
2–3 cups hearty, whole-grain
    breadcrumbs
½ teaspoon garlic powder
1 teaspoon Bragg Liquid Aminos
3 cups shredded zucchini*
1 teaspoon salt
½ teaspoon ground bay leaves
½ teaspoon marjoram
½ teaspoon kelp (optional)
1 tablespoon parsley flakes

Per 1 patty:
    Calories 210
    Protein 14.5 g
    Carbohydrates 24.5 g
    Fiber 7 g
    Fat 6.5 g
    Sodium 530 mg

Steps

1 Combine all ingredients in a large bowl and mix well.

2 Spoon into a preheated non-stick skillet, forming patties with the back of the spoon.

3 Cook 10 minutes on each side.

Makes 12 patties.

*Squeeze juice out of zucchini after shredding. The amount of breadcrumbs needed will depend on the juiciness of the zucchini.

COOK'S TIP

Commercial breadcrumbs can be used, but homemade breadcrumbs are easily made by grinding *Whole Wheat Bread*, page 57, in a food processor and adding garlic powder and a sprinkle of Italian seasonings.

Easy-Peasy Potatoes

Let the kids help you make this recipe.

Ingredients

4 medium baking potatoes
1 cup frozen peas
1 cup *Herb Gravy,* page 169
Salt to taste

Per serving:
    Calories 125
    Protein 3.5 g
    Carbohydrates 21.5 g
    Fiber 4 g
    Fat 3 g
    Sodium 155 mg

HEALTH TIP

Getting your kids to eat vegetables and enjoy other healthy foods is easier if you include them in planning and preparing meals. Involve children in the full meal process, from shopping to cooking, educating them along the way about nutrition and the benefits of certain foods. And make sure to have fun with it too!

Steps

1 Pierce the potatoes with a fork and bake them at 350° for 1 hour. Cool slightly, then slice in half lengthwise.

2 Scoop out the potato into a bowl, leaving ¼ inch of potato next to the skin. Mash the potato with the *Herb Gravy* to a chunky filling. Add the peas and mix. Add salt to taste.

3 Stuff the potato shells with the filling, and place on a baking sheet.

4 Bake at 350° for 20 minutes. Broil the last 1 minute to brown slightly.

Makes 8 halves.

Caramel Corn

The name is a misnomer, in that caramel is really burnt sugar, but this is not. Instead, it is a great combination of whole grain corn and peanut butter with no hydrogenated fats. If the kids help you make it, be sure the "caramel" has cooled just a bit before they dive in and stir it all around!

Ingredients

½ cup unpopped popcorn
¼ cup natural peanut butter
⅓ cup molasses
¼ teaspoon salt

Per ½ cup:
    Calories 75
    Protein 2 g
    Carbohydrates 12.5 g
    Fiber 1.5 g
    Fat 2.5 g
    Sodium 60 mg

Steps

1 Preheat oven to 200°.

2 Pop popcorn in a hot air popper into a large bowl.

3 In a saucepan, combine peanut butter, molasses, and salt.

4 Bring the "caramel" to a boil and stir constantly while it boils for 20 seconds. Immediately pour it over the popcorn and stir well to coat.

5 Bake for 45 minutes. Allow to cool, then place in a plastic bag or airtight container.

Makes 15 cups.

Trail Mix

Whether you're hitting the trail or just having a picnic, this low-fat variety is a hit with kids of all ages!

Ingredients

1 cup Cheerios
½ cup walnuts
½ cup sunflower seeds
¾ cup Spoonsize Shredded Wheat
½ cup carob chips
¾ cup raisins

Per ½ cup:
    Calories 210
    Protein 5 g
    Carbohydrates 25 g
    Fiber 3 g
    Fat 11 g
    Sodium 470 mg

Steps

1 Combine all ingredients in a large bowl and serve.

2 If making ahead, omit the raisins and store in a plastic bag. Add raisins just before serving.

Makes 8 servings.

COOK'S TIP

Get creative with your own recipe … pumpkin seeds, roasted pecans, toasted almonds, slivered or sliced, granola or another cereal, chopped dried fruit of various kinds … there are lots of possibilities!

Banana Popsicles

Better have some of these in the freezer when the grandkids come to visit. Let them in on the fun and get them to help make them.

Ingredients

2 ripe bananas
1 recipe *Carob Fudge Sauce,* page 193
4 popsicle sticks
¾ cup chopped nuts or toasted coconut

Per popsicle:
Calories 320
Protein 6 g
Carbohydrates 42.5 g
Fiber 5.5 g
Fat 17 g
Sodium 105 mg

"Taste and see that the LORD is good!"

—Psalm 34:8

Steps

1 Peel bananas and cut in half. Insert popsicle stick and dip into *Carob Fudge Sauce,* coating completely.

2 Roll gently in chopped nuts or toasted coconut.

3 Freeze on plate covered with waxed paper. Allow to thaw just slightly before serving.

Makes 4 popsicles.

Variation: For frozen *Carob Bon Bons,* use ½-inch banana slices instead of half a banana. Dip slices then freeze them on a waxed paper-covered plate or cookie sheet. Store in a plastic bag.

Dirt Pudding

A total surprise to any newcomer, everyone enjoys the fun! This pudding is most nutritious and very well received.

Ingredients

2 recipes *Carob Pudding,* page 198
¾ cup *Carob Brownie* crumbs,
    page 181
1 small bunch of artificial flowers
1 new ceramic planter (about 5"
    wide by 6" deep)

Per serving:
    Calories 200
    Protein 3.5 g
    Carbohydrates 37 g
    Fiber 3 g
    Fat 5.5 g
    Sodium 115 mg

Steps

1 Crisp the brownie crumbs in a 250° oven for 15 minutes.

2 Cover the hole in the bottom of planter with a few nuts or tape. Pour the *Carob Pudding* into the planter, filling it up within 1 inch from the top.

3 Sprinkle the crisped brownie crumbs over the pudding. It should resemble potting soil.

4 "Plant" the artificial flowers in the pudding and use the *Dirt Pudding* arrangement as the table centerpiece.

5 When it is time for dessert, ask if anyone would like some *Dirt Pudding* and dig in with a serving spoon. Enjoy the laughs and astonished looks on their faces!

Makes 10 servings.

Sides & Sauces

Wild Rice Pilaf recipe on page 160

Aussie Potato Bake

My Australian friend, Robert, was a guest in our home from time to time during his college days. He shared with me how he longed for potatoes like the ones his "mum" used to make. This is what he described and, sure enough, I think it took care of his homesickness, for that meal anyway! Now we all have "Mum's" recipe. It's exceptional!

Ingredients

2 medium-sized sweet potatoes
2 medium-sized white potatoes
13.5-ounce can coconut milk
½ teaspoon salt

Per serving:
    Calories 210
    Protein 3 g
    Carbohydrates 20.5 g
    Fiber 3 g
    Fat 13.5 g
    Sodium 210 mg

Steps

1 Peel and slice potatoes in rounds.

2 Layer in an 8 x 8-inch casserole dish, lightly sprinkling the layers with salt.

3 Pour the coconut milk over the potatoes.

4 Bake at 400° for 45 minutes or until potatoes are tender.

Makes 6 servings.

"Nothing will benefit human health and increase chances of survival for life on earth as much as the evolution to a vegetarian diet."

—Albert Einstein

Oven Roasted Potatoes

Loaded with potassium, roasted potatoes are delicious with only salt, but even more so with these added ingredients.

Ingredients

3 large Russet potatoes
    or 5 medium red potatoes
1 tablespoon olive oil
½ teaspoon garlic powder
2 tablespoons Bragg Liquid Aminos
    or 1 teaspoon salt
½ teaspoon Italian seasonings
    or 1 tablespoon fresh rosemary
1 teaspoon onion powder
½ teaspoon paprika
2 tablespoons nutritional yeast flakes

Per serving:
    Calories 160
    Protein 4.5 g
    Carbohydrates 34 g
    Fiber 2.5 g
    Fat 1.5 g
    Sodium 230 mg

Steps

1. If using Russet potatoes, slice each potato into 8 wedges and place them in a large casserole dish. Cut red potatoes into 1½-inch cubes.

2. Drizzle and sprinkle with remaining ingredients, then toss to coat potatoes.

3. Roast at 450° for 30 minutes or until tender.

Makes 6 servings.

Roasted Root Vegetables

Roasting brings out the sweetness and rich flavor of these fall and winter veggies. Other vegetables can be roasted as well, or you can use a variation of those listed. Roasted vegetables are a wonderful addition to a holiday meal.

Ingredients

2 medium carrots
3 medium parsnips
2 medium turnips
2 medium red potatoes
1 large sweet potato
1 large onion
½ teaspoon salt
1 tablespoon olive oil
1 teaspoon dried thyme

Per serving:
  Calories 90
  Protein 2 g
  Carbohydrates 18 g
  Fiber 3.5 g
  Fat 1.5 g
  Sodium 125 mg

Steps

1 Preheat oven to 450°.

2 Peel and cut root vegetables into ¾-inch chunks. Spread single layer onto a large baking sheet.

3 Cut onion into chunks and separate into 2-layer pieces. Add to vegetables.

4 Drizzle vegetables with olive oil and sprinkle with salt and thyme.

5 Stir to coat well.

6 Roast uncovered for 45 minutes.
Makes 12 servings.

Eat for strength!
  —Ecclesiastes 10:17

Polenta

A versatile side dish, polenta can go sweet or savory and is absolutely delicious.

Ingredients

1 cup polenta (coarse grain cornmeal)
4 cups water
½ teaspoon salt

Per ½ cup:
Calories 60
Protein 1.5 g
Carbohydrates 13.5 g
Fiber 1.5 g
Fat .5 g
Sodium 175 mg

COOK'S TIP

For a healthy version of cheese grits, serve straight from the saucepan and top with *Healthy Melty Cheese,* page 171.

Steps

1 Combine polenta and water in a medium saucepan.

2 Cook on medium-high heat, stirring continually with a whisk until polenta becomes thick.

3 Continue cooking on very low heat for 30 minutes.

4 Pour into a glass loaf pan and allow to cool. If using a metal loaf pan, line with plastic wrap. Place in refrigerator to chill.

5 After it becomes firm, turn out onto cutting board. Slice into ¼-inch slices.

6 Reheat in oil-sprayed skillet or grill pan until it begins to slightly brown.

Makes 7 servings.

Baked Brown Rice

After discovering baking rice in the oven, I have never returned to the stovetop method. This rice is perfect every time! Millet also can be baked in the oven with the same proportions of grain to water and salt.

Ingredients

3 cups brown rice
6 cups water
1 teaspoon salt

Per ½ cup:
    Calories 130
    Protein 2.5 g
    Carbohydrates 27 g
    Fiber 1.2 g
    Fat 1 g
    Sodium 145 mg

Steps

1 Place all ingredients in a 9 x 13-inch casserole dish.

2 Cover and bake at 350° for 1½ hours.

Makes 16 servings.

COOK'S TIP

Both rice and millet can be frozen for later use. It is helpful to measure and mark the freezer bag with the amount. If using cooked rice in a recipe, remember to adjust for salt if using salted rice.

Wild Rice Pilaf

An excellent accompaniment to Baked Tofu, page 131, this pilaf could be made with brown rice, whole wheat couscous, or quinoa.

Ingredients

8 ounces Lundberg Wild Blend rice
3 cups water
½ teaspoon salt
1 cup chopped onion
1 clove fresh garlic, pressed
1 small zucchini, diced
1 carrot, sliced
1 tablespoon olive oil
1 tablespoon Bragg Liquid Aminos
1 teaspoon dried basil
1 tablespoon parsley flakes

Per ½ cup:
    Calories 130
    Protein 4.5 g
    Carbohydrates 23 g
    Fiber 2 g
    Fat 2.5 g
    Sodium 310 mg

Steps

1 Cook rice according to package. Allow to cool.

2 Steam onion, garlic, zucchini, and carrot in a small amount of water in a large saucepan.

3 Add cooked rice and remaining ingredients and toss to mix.

Makes 6 servings.

COOK'S TIP

Varry the veggies according to your preference; broccoli and red bell pepper, and edamame and yellow squash are good combinations. Think color; think nutrition.

Cauliflower au Gratin

Your family will not believe this recipe has no cheese in it. It is reminiscent of a gruyere cheese casserole that I was served in France, and it is just as tasty. Tahini is the key ingredient that gives this dish a wonderful, cheesy flavor.

Ingredients

1 head of cauliflower
2½ cups water
¼ cup rinsed, raw cashews
1 tablespoon lemon juice
¼ cup nutritional yeast flakes
2 tablespoons tahini
1 teaspoon onion powder
¼ teaspoon garlic powder
¼ cup cornstarch
1¼ teaspoons salt
1 jar pearl onions

Per serving:
    Calories 130
    Protein 6 g
    Carbohydrates 16 g
    Fiber 5 g
    Fat 6 g
    Sodium 460 mg

Steps

1 Core the cauliflower and cut it into 2-inch pieces, then place them in a large steamer. Steam until crisp tender.

2 Bring 1½ cups of the water to a boil in a saucepan.

3 Liquefy the remaining ingredients, and include the remaining 1 cup of water, in the blender.

4 Pour blended mixture into boiling water and continue cooking until thick.

5 Arrange cauliflower and pearl onions in a large casserole dish. Pour sauce over vegetables and serve. Garnish with fresh parsley and paprika.

Makes 8 servings.

Southern Side of Squash

This is one vegetable I like "cooked to death." Please notice I have left out the bacon grease!

Ingredients

4 medium yellow summer squash
1 large onion
½ teaspoon salt
1 tablespoon olive oil

Per serving:
    Calories 70
    Protein 2.5 g
    Carbohydrates 10.5 g
    Fiber 2.5 g
    Fat 2.5 g
    Sodium 300 mg

Steps

1 Slice squash into ¼-inch rounds and onion into half-rounds.

2 Coat the bottom of a large skillet with the olive oil. Add squash, onions, and salt and sauté for 5 minutes. Cover.

3 Turn down heat, allowing squash to simmer for about 30 minutes, until tender.

4 Chop squash and onions into ½- to 1-inch pieces with a firm spatula.

5 Continue cooking an additional 10 minutes.

Makes 4 servings.

COOK'S TIP

Serve with fresh or frozen lima beans (known as "butter beans" in the South), cooked until tender, and with garden fresh tomatoes and corn on the cob.

Summer Squash Bake

Baking vegetables minimizes steps in the kitchen and maximizes nutrient retention. When the garden is producing squash and onions, this is perfect for a potluck.

Ingredients

4 medium summer squash
1 large onion
1 recipe *Healthy Melty Cheese,*
    page 171

Per serving:
    Calories 130
    Protein 5.5 g
    Carbohydrates 16 g
    Fiber 3.5 g
    Fat 6 g
    Sodium 410 mg

Steps

1 Preheat oven to 400°.

2 Slice squash and onions and arrange in 9 x 13-inch casserole dish.

3 Pour *Healthy Melty Cheese* over vegetables.

4 Bake for 30 minutes.

Makes 8 servings.

Pan-Fried Okra

Another Southern favorite, but without the health risk of the deep-fried version or the dreaded "slime factor!"

Ingredients

20 okra pods
½ cup cornmeal
2 tablespoons whole wheat flour
½ teaspoon salt
2 tablespoons light olive oil

Per serving:
  Calories 145
  Protein 3 g
  Carbohydrates 18g
  Fiber 2.5 g
  Fat 7.5 g
  Sodium 300 mg

Steps

1 Slice okra into ½-inch rounds.

2 Put okra and dry ingredients into a plastic bag and shake well to coat evenly.

3 Place in preheated skillet with the oil. Brown for 10 minutes over medium heat, turning with spatula every couple of minutes. Reduce heat, cover, and continue cooking for 5 more minutes, turning okra after 3 minutes.

4 Remove lid and continue browning until crisp, another 5 minutes. Serve hot.

Makes 4 servings.

Fresh Collard Greens

Collards, kale, and turnips greens are rich sources of calcium, as well as folate, and should be served at least weekly. No Southern meal is complete without them!

Ingredients

10 cups fresh collards
2 cups water
1 teaspoon onion powder
½ teaspoon garlic powder
½ teaspoon salt
Bakon yeast (optional)

Per ½ cup:
 Calories 25
 Protein 2 g
 Carbohydrates 5 g
 Fiber 2.5 g
 Fat .5 g
 Sodium 150 mg
 Calcium 100 mg
 Folate 100 mcg

Steps

1 Wash and chop desired amount of collards and place in a large saucepan with about 1½ inches of water in bottom of pan.

2 Bring to a boil over medium-high heat. Cover and reduce heat and simmer for 30 to 45 minutes or less, just until tender. It will depend on how tender the greens are.

3 Add seasonings. For those who enjoy a bacon-like seasoning, Bakon yeast, which is dried torula yeast with a hickory smoke flavor can be added, but these greens are still very delicious, with the simple ingredients included.

4 Serve with lemon juice, if desired.

Makes 6 servings.

HEALTH TIP

Dark green leafy vegetables and prepared dried beans are excellent sources of calcium, the mineral that helps us build a strong skeletal system. Weight-bearing exercise also helps to strengthen the bones. Include walking, gardening, or other physical activity most days of the week to help keep your bones strong.

Green Bean Amandine

A welcomed change from green bean casserole, these beans are a "snap" to make!

Ingredients

4 cups fresh or frozen green beans
½ teaspoon Vegesal or salt
1½ teaspoons dill weed
¼ cup sliced almonds

Per ¾ cup:
    Calories 80
    Protein 3.5 g
    Carbohydrates 7.5 g
    Fiber 3.5 g
    Fat 5 g
    Sodium 200 mg

COOK'S TIP

A drizzle of olive oil can be added if desired.

Steps

1 Steam green beans until tender, about 10 minutes. The beans can be left whole or cut into thirds.

2 Toss with dill weed and Vegesal.

3 Toast almonds for 10 minutes at 250°, and add them just before serving.

Makes 6 servings.

Sweet Potato Soufflé

Not really a soufflé, this dish is a must-have at every Thanksgiving dinner. It is rich in beta-carotene and topped with walnuts, giving it a wonderful blend of taste and texture.

Ingredients

4 medium sweet potatoes
2 teaspoons vanilla extract
2 teaspoons honey
¼ teaspoon salt
1 teaspoon ground coriander
¼ cup soy or nut milk
1 tablespoon molasses
¼ cup walnuts, chopped

Per ½ cup:
- Calories 95
- Protein 2 g
- Carbohydrates 16 g
- Fiber 2.5 g
- Fat 2.5 g
- Sodium 85 mg

Steps

1 Wash sweet potatoes and pierce with a fork.

2 Bake until soft and juices are appearing (350° for about an hour).

3 Cool, peel, and mash sweet potatoes and add remaining ingredients. A food processor works well.

4 Pour into a casserole dish and top with chopped walnuts.

5 Bake at 350° for 30 minutes.

Makes 6 servings.

HEALTH TIP

When we look at sweet potatoes, we see beta-carotene, but they are also good sources of calcium, potassium, and fiber. Sweet potato recipes made with healthful ingredients make the perfect side or dessert.

Fresh Cranberry Relish

Tangy and festive, this is the perfect accompaniment to a holiday dinner. Leftover relish makes a good topping for toast that has been spread with almond butter.

Ingredients

3 cups fresh cranberries
1 large apple
6 large dried apricots
½ cup frozen white grape
    cranberry or white grape
    raspberry juice concentrate

Per ¼ cup:
    Calories 65
    Protein .5 g
    Carbohydrates 16 g
    Fiber 3 g
    Fat 0 g
    Sodium 2 mg

"Bless the LORD, O my soul... Who satisfies your mouth with good things, so that your youth is renewed like the eagle's."

—*Psalm 103:1, 5*

Steps

1 Process cranberries in food processor until chopped fine, then transfer to a mixing bowl.

2 Core and peel apple and then cut into chunks. Place in food processor and chop fine. Add to cranberries.

3 Use a knife to dice dried apricots into small pieces. Add to bowl.

4 Add juice concentrate and mix well.

5 Serve chilled with a savory entrée for a festive holiday meal.

Makes 8 servings.

Herb Gravy

For many, the best part of a "meat and potatoes" meal is the gravy, and this one is something to write home about. In addition, it can be used very successfully to replace butter and milk in mashed potatoes. Serve with Millet Loaf, *page 126, or* Holiday Loaf, *page 125, for a special meal any time of year.*

Ingredients

½ cup rinsed, raw cashews
2 cups water
4½ teaspoons cornstarch
1½ teaspoons onion powder
½ teaspoon garlic powder
1½ teaspoons Bragg Liquid Aminos
½ teaspoon lemon juice
½ teaspoon dried basil or
    1 tablespoon fresh basil
Pinch of rosemary
½ teaspoon salt
¼ teaspoon parsley flakes or a sprig
    of fresh parsley

Per ¼ cup:
    Calories 70
    Protein 2 g
    Carbohydrates 4.5 g
    Fiber .5 g
    Fat 5.5 g
    Sodium 150 mg

Steps

1 Bring 1 cup of the water to a boil in a medium saucepan.

2 Blend remaining ingredients, except parsley, until very smooth in the blender.

3 Pour blended mixture into the boiling water and stir with a whisk until thickened. The gravy will thicken further as it cools. Garnish with parsley.

Makes 2½ cups.

"Those who persevere in obedience to the laws of health will reap the reward in health of body and health of mind."

    —Ellen G. White

Onion Rings

Fried onion rings might naturally be vegetarian, but the damaging high fat will likely negate any benefit. This version is absolutely delicious and completely healthy. Eggplant can also be prepared in this manner as well. Serve it with tartar sauce.

Ingredients

3 large onions
1 recipe *Tofu Mayonnaise,* page 74
3 cups seasoned whole grain bread crumbs

Per 6 onion rings:
   Calories 190
   Protein 12 g
   Carbohydrates 19 g
   Fiber 4 g
   Fat 8.5 g
   Sodium 375 mg

COOK'S TIP

Make homemade seasoned breadcrumbs by grinding *Whole Wheat Bread,* page 57, in a food processor and adding garlic powder and a sprinkle of Italian seasonings.

Steps

1 Slice onions and separate into rings.

2 Thin out mayonnaise in a small bowl with a little water, about 2 tablespoons.

3 Dip onion rings in mayonnaise with one fork, then use another fork to place on a plateful of breadcrumbs. Turn to coat evenly.

4 Bake on non-stick cookie sheet at 325° for 20 to 25 minutes.

Makes about 42.

"Do you not know that your body is the temple of the Holy Spirit who is in you, whom you have from God, and you are not your own? For you were bought at a price; therefore glorify God in your body and in your spirit, which are God's."

—1 Corinthians 6:19, 20

Healthy Melty Cheese

This sauce so closely resembles the real thing, you can fool anybody. Considering that it is very low in fat and cholesterol free, it can be enjoyed often.

Ingredients

¼ cup rinsed, raw cashews
4-ounce jar pimiento, drained
1 tablespoon lemon juice
¼ cup nutritional yeast flakes
2 tablespoons tahini
1 teaspoon onion powder
¼ teaspoon garlic powder
3 tablespoons cornstarch
1¼ teaspoons salt
¼ teaspoon celery seed (optional)
2½ cups water

Per ¼ cup:
    Calories 60
    Protein 2.5 g
    Carbohydrates 6 g
    Fiber 1.5 g
    Fat 3.5 g
    Sodium 250 mg

Steps

1 Bring 1½ cups of the water to a boil in a saucepan.

2 Liquefy the remaining ingredients including the remaining 1 cup of water, in the blender until smooth.

3 Pour blended mixture into boiling water and continue cooking until thick.

4 Serve immediately over broccoli, pasta, baked potato, or toast, or you can use in a casserole. It's also perfect for nachos!

Makes 3 cups.

Spaghetti Sauce

The secret to making classic Italian sauce is using crushed tomatoes. Purchase only an Italian brand for the desired texture. When you start with quality crushed tomatoes, arriving at an authentic sauce is simple.

Ingredients

1½ teaspoon olive oil
1 cup diced onion
2 cloves garlic, pressed
28-ounce can crushed tomatoes
14.4-ounce can diced tomatoes
1 teaspoon salt
1 teaspoon basil
½ teaspoon lemon juice
1 teaspoon olive oil
½ teaspoon oregano
1 teaspoon honey

Per ½ cup:
Calories 40
Protein 1 g
Carbohydrates 7 g
Fiber 1.5 g
Fat 1 g
Sodium 350 mg

Steps

1 Sauté onions and garlic in oil.

2 Add remaining ingredients and simmer for 10 minutes.

Makes 6 cups.

COOK'S TIP

This recipe calls for diced tomatoes for the sake of convenience. I prefer whole tomatoes that you crush with your hands.

"By eating the right food, we can keep our hearts healthy."

—T. Colin Campbell, PhD

Italian Marinade

Perfect for grilled tofu or shish kabobs. Also is an excellent marinade for roasted vegetables.

Ingredients

½ cup olive oil
½ cup water
⅓ cup lemon juice
4 teaspoons honey
1 tablespoon Bragg Liquid Aminos
2 teaspoons parsley flakes
2 large cloves pressed garlic
1 teaspoon onion powder
½ teaspoon oregano
¼ teaspoon salt

Per 2 tablespoons:
    Calories 65
    Protein .5 g
    Carbohydrates 3 g
    Fiber .1 g
    Fat 6 g
    Sodium 100 mg

Steps

1 Combine all ingredients in a jar and shake to mix, or pulse briefly in the blender.

2 Marinate tofu, vegetables or reconstituted Soy Curls for about 30 minutes before grilling, broiling, or roasting.

Makes 1½ cups.

COOK'S TIP

If using the blender to mix, pressing the garlic cloves will be unnecessary.

Béarnaise Sauce

Usually considered a sauce for meat, this béarnaise sauce is a wonderful accompaniment for Baked Tofu, *page 131, or steamed vegetables.*

Ingredients

2 tablespoons light olive oil
2 tablespoons white flour
1 cup plain Silk soymilk
1 tablespoon lemon juice
½ teaspoon onion powder
¼ teaspoon garlic powder
1/16 teaspoon turmeric
¼ teaspoon salt

Per 2 tablespoons:
  Calories 45
  Protein 1 g
  Carbohydrates 2.5 g
  Fiber .5 g
  Fat 3.5 g
  Sodium 70 mg

Steps

1 Heat oil over medium heat in a saucepan. Add flour and stir to make a roux (paste).

2 Gradually add milk, stirring constantly over heat to avoid lumping.

3 Add remaining ingredients and continue to stir until smooth. Serve immediately.

Makes a little over 1 cup.

COOK'S TIP

If preferred, all ingredients can be combined in the blender. Whiz for 15 seconds, then cook on medium heat until thick, stirring constantly.

Oriental Glaze

This glaze is the finishing touch to an Asian vegetable stir fry. Adjust the Bragg Liquid Aminos to your liking and your sodium requirements.

Ingredients

2 cups water or pineapple juice
¼ cup cornstarch
¼ cup Bragg Liquid Aminos
1 teaspoon garlic powder or
    2 cloves sliced fresh garlic
1 teaspoon lemon juice (optional)

Per ¼ cup (using pineapple juice):
    Calories 45
    Protein .5 g
    Carbohydrates 10.5 g
    Fiber .2 g
    Fat 0 g
    Sodium 260 mg

Steps

1 Pour 1½ cups water or juice in medium saucepan and bring to boil.

2 Mix remaining ½ cup water or juice with the other ingredients in a cup or small bowl.

3 Add cornstarch mixture to boiling liquid. Stir constantly with whisk until thickened.

4 Pour over steamed vegetables and mix for *Vegetable Stir Fry,* page 134.

Makes 2½ cups.

Spanish Rice

Another authentic recipe from Zinia, the flavor achieved warrants the effort.

Ingredients

1 cup fresh or frozen corn
½ cup red and/or green pepper, chopped
1 medium onion, diced
½ cup fresh cilantro, chopped
2–3 garlic cloves, thinly sliced
2–3 teaspoons tomato paste or purée
2–3 teaspoons olive oil
3 cups short grain brown rice
5½ cups water
1½ teaspoons salt

Per ½ cup:
 Calories 150
 Protein 3.5 g
 Carbohydrates 30 g
 Fiber 3 g
 Fat 2 g
 Sodium 240 mg

Steps

1 In a large, heavy-bottom saucepan, sauté corn, pepper, onion, cilantro, garlic, and tomato paste in the olive oil.

2 Add rice, water, and salt.

3 Cover and cook for 45 minutes on low heat. Gently fluff with a fork.

Makes 16 servings.

COOK'S TIP

Here's a shortcut method: Sauté ingredients in #1. Add 4 cups *Baked Brown Rice,* page 159. Salt to taste and add more tomato purée if desired. Mix well and heat through. Quick and easy!

Picadillo Sauce

A fancy salsa straight from Puerto Rico.

Ingredients

½ cup chopped onion
½ cup chopped green pepper
1 stalk celery, finely diced
½ cup fresh cilantro leaves,
    sliced thin
1 teaspoon garlic powder
½ teaspoon cumin
1 cup canned diced tomatoes
Pinch of salt
1 teaspoon sweetener
1 teaspoon cornstarch
½ cup water

Per ¼ cup:
    Calories 25
    Protein .5 g
    Carbohydrates 3.5 g
    Fiber .5 g
    Fat 1 g
    Sodium 50 mg

COOK'S TIP

If serving with burritos, garnish
the dish with sliced black olives
and shredded soy cheese.

Steps

1 In large skillet, sauté onion, green pepper, and cilantro leaves in oil or cover and steam in water just until tender.

2 Add garlic powder, cumin, tomatoes, and sweetener to the sautéed vegetables and bring to a boil.

3 Dissolve cornstarch in the water, pour into the vegetable mixture.

4 Reduce heat and continue cooking for 2 to 3 minutes, stirring constantly until thickened. Serve hot over burritos.

Makes 3 cups.

Cakes & Bakes

Tofu Cheesecake recipe on page 185

Banana Date Cookies

These cookies are naturally sweet and delicious, and they are especially good right out of the oven and cooled just a bit.

Ingredients

3 ripe bananas, mashed
1 cup chopped dates
½ cup walnuts, chopped
2 cups quick oats
1 cup unsweetened coconut
1 cup raisins
1 teaspoon vanilla extract
½ teaspoon salt

Per cookie:
  Calories 170
  Protein 2.5 g
  Carbohydrates 21.5 g
  Fiber 3.5 g
  Fat 9 g
  Sodium 55 mg

Steps

1 Preheat oven to 350°.

2 Mash bananas with a fork on a plate. Combine with all ingredients in a mixing bowl and mix well.

3 Drop by tablespoons onto non-stick cookie sheet. Flatten with a fork and bake for 25 minutes.

Makes 24 cookies.

COOK'S TIP

These are best served within several hours from the oven. The next day, reheat to crisp before serving.

"Drugs and surgery don't cure the diseases that kill most Americans."

—T. Colin Campbell, PhD

Happy Cookies

Chock-full of omega-3 essential fatty acid, these delicious cookies might even aid in lifting depression! See Dr. Neil Nedley's book, Depression: The Way Out, *for a complete lifestyle program designed to combat depression.*

Ingredients

2½ cups English walnuts
⅔ cup maple syrup
1 tablespoon light olive oil
2 teaspoons vanilla extract
1 teaspoon salt
⅓ cup flax meal
½ cup whole wheat flour
⅓ cup dairy-free carob chips

Per 1 cookie:
  Calories 140
  Protein 2.5 g
  Carbohydrates 11.5 g
  Fiber 10 g
  Fat 10 g
  Sodium 100 mg

Steps

1 Preheat oven to 350°.

2 Grind 1½ cups of the walnuts in the blender or food processor, leaving some coarsely ground. Pour into a mixing bowl.

3 Blend remaining 1 cup of walnuts with the maple syrup, oil, vanilla extract, and salt in a blender. Mixture should be smooth and creamy.

4 Add blended mixture to the ground walnuts. Add remaining ingredients and mix well.

5 Form cookies by placing slightly more than 1 tablespoon of batter on non-stick cookie sheet. Flatten with the back of a spoon coated with oil. (Using a small scoop sprayed with oil also works well.)

6 Bake for 12 minutes. Watch closely as oven temperatures can vary.

Makes 24 cookies.

COOK'S TIP

Raisins are a wonderful substitute for the carob chips, or get creative and add other chopped dried fruits.

Carob Brownies

Finally, a vegan brownie that is rich and moist. It's perfect for hot fudge cake, using Tofutti or homemade vegan ice cream, of course!

Ingredients

⅔ cup whole wheat flour
½ cup carob powder
1 tablespoon powdered coffee
　　substitute (Roma)
⅓ cup Sucanat or brown sugar
1 tablespoon Ener-G baking powder
　　or 1½ teaspoons Rumford
　　baking powder
1 cup walnuts, chopped
¾ cup soy or nut milk
½ teaspoon salt
1 teaspoon vanilla extract
⅓ cup honey

Per brownie:
　　Calories 235
　　Protein 4 g
　　Carbohydrates 38 g
　　Fiber 3.2 g
　　Fat 9 g
　　Sodium 150 mg

COOK'S TIP

For an excellent pudding topping, crumble several brownies and spread onto cookie sheet. Crisp in 250° oven for 20 minutes.

Steps

1 Preheat oven to 400°. Prepare 8 x 8-inch pan with nonstick spray.

2 Measure all dry ingredients, except walnuts, into one bowl and wet ingredients into another. Add walnuts to wet ingredients.

3 When oven is hot, mix together dry and wet ingredients. Stir quickly, being careful not to stir out bubbles. (Ener-G baking powder is moisture activated, while Rumford is heat activated). Place in oven immediately.

4 Bake at 400° for 5 minutes, then reduce heat to 350° and continue baking for 25 minutes. Cool and top with *Carob Fudge Sauce*, page 193.

Makes 9 large brownies.

Pineapple Right-Side-Up Cake

Here is a recipe with quite a few steps, but it's easy to get it right! A luscious, creamy combination, this cake will get rave reviews.

Ingredients

Cake:
1 cup whole wheat flour
1 cup unbleached white flour
2 tablespoons Ener-G baking
     powder or 1 tablespoon
     Rumford baking powder
¾ teaspoon salt
½ cup light olive oil
½ cup honey
1 cup pineapple juice
1 teaspoon vanilla extract
½ teaspoon coconut extract

Topping:
6 ounces extra firm silken tofu
13.5-ounce can coconut milk
3 tablespoons sweetener
⅛ teaspoon salt
1 teaspoon vanilla extract
2 teaspoons Instant Clear Jel

To assemble, you will also need:
20-ounce can crushed pineapple,
     in juice
⅓ cup toasted slivered almonds
¼ cup diced dried apricots

Per serving:
   Calories 425
   Protein 8.5 g
   Carbohydrates 54 g
   Fiber 4 g
   Fat 21.5 g
   Sodium 215 mg

Steps

Cake:
1 Preheat oven to 375°.

2 Combine flours, baking powder, and salt in a medium bowl and stir with a whisk.

3 Combine remaining liquid ingredients in another bowl and mix well.

4 Pour liquid mixture over dry ingredients and mix well, being careful not to stir bubbles out.

5 Bake in oiled and floured 9-inch round pan for 45 minutes.

Topping:
1 Place all ingredients, except Instant Clear Jel, in blender. Blend until smooth.

2 Sprinkle Instant Clear Jel into blender while blending mixture on medium speed. Chill for 2 to 3 hours, until thick.

3 Drain ½ cup juice from the pineapple.

4 Spoon pineapple over cake, allowing some juice to penetrate the cake.

5 Top with coconut milk topping, toasted almonds, and apricots.

Makes 12 servings.

German Carob Cake

Did you ever feel like you were "going international" when serving German chocolate cake? Turns out, a homemaker in Dallas, Texas, developed the recipe — and its name comes from the sweet chocolate baking bar developed for Baker's Chocolate Company in 1852 by Sam German. For most of us, it's the frosting that is the signature trait of this old favorite, and this version is delicious without the butter, eggs, and milk. Walnuts are used instead of pecans as they maintain a crispier texture. The carob cake recipe is a great stand-in for the German chocolate cake. Carob is already sweet, like Mr. German's chocolate bar, so it's the perfect healthy alternative. This cake is rich, so serve it with a meal that is lower in fat.

Ingredients

Cake:
3⅓ cups whole wheat pastry flour
2 tablespoons Ener-G baking
    powder or 1 tablespoon
    Rumford baking powder
2 cups Sucanat
    or turbinado sugar
1 teaspoon salt
6 tablespoons carob powder
1 tablespoon powdered coffee
    substitute (Roma)
⅔ cup light olive oil
2 cups water
2 teaspoons vanilla extract

Steps

Cake:

1 Preheat oven to 350°.

2 Mix dry ingredients in one bowl and wet ingredients in another.

3 Combine liquid to dry ingredients and mix until moist and most lumps have disappeared.

4 Pour into two 9-inch cake pans and bake immediately. Bake until toothpick inserted in center comes out clean, 35 to 40 minutes.

"Whether you eat or drink, or whatever you do, do all to the glory of God."

—1 Corinthians 10:31

Recipe continues on next page …

Ingredients

Coconut Walnut Frosting:
2 cups vanilla Silk soy milk
½ cup Sucanat
½ cup chopped dates
1 teaspoon vanilla extract
¼ teaspoon salt
4 teaspoons cornstarch
2 cups unsweetened, flake coconut
1 cup English walnuts, coarsely
    chopped

Per 2 x 2-inch piece:
    Calories 430
    Protein 6 g
    Carbohydrates 40 g
    Fiber 7.5 g
    Fat 28.5 g
    Sodium 135 mg

Steps

Frosting:

1 Blend all ingredients, except the coconut and walnuts, in the blender until smooth.

2 Pour mixture into saucepan and cook over medium-high heat, stirring constantly until thickened.

3 Add coconut and walnuts and stir to mix.

4 Allow to cool before spreading on cake.

Makes 16 servings.

COOK'S TIP

This cake is also excellent with *Carob Fudge Sauce,* page 193, or *Berry Fruit Sauce,* page 189; or to make *Black Forest Cake,* layer with *Carob Mocha Mousse,* page 200; fresh, pitted dark cherries; and frost with *Coconut Whipped Cream,* page 192.

Tofu Cheesecake

Light and beautiful, this cheesecake makes for a wonderful ending to any meal. Serve with Strawberry Jam, *page 190, or* Berry Fruit Sauce, *page 189.*

Ingredients

20-ounce can crushed pineapple, in juice
3½ tablespoons cornstarch
½ cup rinsed, raw cashews
2 12.3-ounce packages silken tofu, extra firm
½ cup pineapple juice concentrate
⅓ cup honey
Rind of ½ lemon
    or ½ teaspoon lemon extract
½ teaspoon salt

Per serving:
    Calories 185
    Protein 8 g
    Carbohydrates 21 g
    Fiber 1 g
    Fat 8 g
    Sodium 100 mg

COOK'S TIP

Fresh fanned strawberries are a beautiful garnish for this dessert. Make ⅛-inch thick cuts toward the cap of the strawberry, then fan open.

Steps

1 Preheat oven to 350°.

2 Combine crushed pineapple, cornstarch, and cashews in blender and blend smooth.

3 Add remaining ingredients and blend again.

4 Pour into prepared crumb crust in 9 x 13-inch casserole dish or spring-form pan.

5 Bake for 45 minutes and allow to cool.

6 Chill and serve with *Strawberry Jam,* page 190, and fruit garnish or *Berry Fruit Sauce.*

Makes 12 servings.

"Have you found honey?
Eat only as much as you need."

—*Proverbs 25:16*

Vegan Tiramisu

Yes, there are a lot of steps to this version of the exquisite Italian dessert, but they are steps you will be glad you took!

Ingredients

Espresso Syrup:
2½ tablespoons powdered coffee
    substitute (Roma or Postum)
1½ tablespoons carob powder
3 tablespoons water
1½ tablespoons maple syrup
1½ teaspoons vanilla extract
2 dashes salt

Custard:
12.3 ounces silken tofu, extra firm
Two 13.5-ounce cans coconut milk
¼ cup turbinado sugar
½ teaspoon stevia powder
⅛ teaspoon salt
2 teaspoons vanilla extract
1 teaspoon *Espresso Syrup*
2 tablespoons Instant Clear Jel or
    cornstarch

Cake:
½ cup whole wheat pastry flour
½ cup unbleached flour
2 teaspoons Ener-G baking powder
    or 1 teaspoon Rumford baking
    powder
½ teaspoon salt
3 tablespoons turbinado sugar
½ teaspoon stevia powder
⅓ cup white grape juice
    concentrate
⅓ cup water
1 teaspoon vanilla extract
3 tablespoons light olive oil

Steps

Espresso Syrup:
1 Combine all ingredients in a small saucepan and bring to boil. Allow to boil for 30 seconds. Cool.

Custard:
1 Place all ingredients, except the Instant Clear Jel or cornstarch, in the blender and liquefy.

2 If using cornstarch, pour ½ cup of the blended mixture into a small bowl. Add the cornstarch and stir to mix well.

3 Heat the remaining custard in a large saucepan, stirring occasionally. When it begins to steam, add the cornstarch mixture and stir continually until it thickens. Allow to cool.

4 If using Instant Clear Jel, sprinkle it into the custard mixture gradually while the blended mixture is moving on medium speed.

5 Refrigerate the custard for 45 minutes to chill and thicken.

Cake:
1 Preheat oven to 350°.

2 Combine flours, baking powder, sugar, stevia powder, and salt in medium bowl and stir with a whisk to mix.

Per serving:
    Calories 210
    Protein 3.5 g
    Carbohydrates 20 g
    Fiber 1 g
    Fat 13.5 g
    Sodium 105 mg

COOK'S TIP

In cake and custard, stevia powder can be replaced with 3 tablespoons more turbinado sugar. Also, *Vegan Tiramisu* can be assembled in two layers in an 8 x 8-inch pan.

Steps (continued)

Cake (continued):

3 Combine juice concentrate, water, vanilla, and oil in another bowl and mix well.

4 Pour liquid mixture over dry ingredients and stir to mix, being careful not to stir bubbles out if using Ener-G baking powder.

5 Spread batter into an oil-sprayed 9 x 13-inch pan. The layer will be quite thin. Bake for 20 minutes.

6 After the cake has cooled, cut it into four strips for ease of handling, and then remove them from the pan. Wash this pan so it will be ready to assemble the recipe.

To Assemble:

1 Pour all but 2 tablespoons of the *Espresso Syrup* into the bottom of the 9 x 13-inch pan. Tilt the pan to coat the bottom. Place the cake strips back into the pan.

2 Drizzle or brush the remaining *Espresso Syrup* on the cake. Place 2 tablespoons of carob powder in a tea strainer and dust the top of the cake.

3 Pour the chilled custard over the cake and refrigerate for about 30 minutes, until it begins to set.

4 Liberally dust the top of the *Vegan Tiramisu* with more of the carob powder. Place in refrigerator and continue to chill until firm.

Makes 15 servings.

Sweet Toppings

Carob Fudge Sauce recipe on page 193

Berry Fruit Sauce

On Tofu Cheesecake, page 185, Carob Cake, page 183, Belgian Waffles, page 44, or French Toast, page 46, this sauce is beautiful and absolutely delicious.

Ingredients

12-ounce can white grape raspberry juice concentrate
1 can water
4 tablespoons cornstarch
16-ounce package frozen mixed berries, raspberries, or blueberries

Per ¼ cup:
    Calories 40
    Protein .2 g
    Carbohydrates 9 g
    Fiber .5 g
    Fat 0 g
    Sodium 2 mg

Steps

1 Dissolve cornstarch in ½ cup of the water.

2 Heat juice and remaining water in saucepan until boiling.

3 Add cornstarch mixture and stir over medium-high heat until thickened.

4 Add frozen fruit, stir, and remove from heat.

Makes 20 servings.

Pictured with *Belgian Waffles* on page 44 and with *Tofu Cheesecake* on page 185.

COOK'S TIP

Any flavor of juice concentrate can be used. Fresh fruit can also be used, of course. You might even want to try:
   White Grape Peach juice with frozen or fresh peaches
   White grape cranberry with fresh sliced strawberries

"I give you every seed-bearing plant on the face of the whole earth and every tree that has fruit with seed in it. They will be yours for food."

—Genesis 1:29 (NIV)

Strawberry Jam

An excellent breakfast spread or topping for Tofu Cheesecake, page 185, garnished with fresh sliced strawberries. Easy to whip up, this topping can be enjoyed year round, as frozen berries work well.

Ingredients

2½ cups fresh or frozen
   strawberries
½ cup pitted dates or dried
   pineapple

Per 2 tablespoons:
   Calories 60
   Protein 1 g
   Carbohydrates 16 g
   Fiber 2.5 g
   Fat 0 g
   Sodium 0 mg

Steps

1 Thaw strawberries if frozen. Purée the berries in a blender.

2 If dates are not soft, place in small amount of water and steam in the microwave or on the stove.

3 Combine with strawberries in the blender and blend smooth. Chill to thicken. Keep refrigerated.

Makes 1½ cups.

"The more we depend upon the fresh fruit as it is plucked from the tree, the greater will be the blessing."

—*Ellen G. White*

Tofu Whipped Topping

What a wonderful way to use tofu! This topping is especially enjoyable in a parfait or layered dessert, such as Carob Delight, *page 199.*

Ingredients

12.3 ounces silken tofu, extra firm
3 tablespoons honey
¼ cup rinsed, raw cashews
¼ cup water
½ teaspoon coconut or vanilla extract
½ teaspoon lemon juice
⅛ teaspoon salt

Steps

1 Blend all ingredients in blender until smooth.

2 Chill before serving.

Makes 2¼ cups.

Per ¼ cup:
   Calories 80
   Protein 4 g
   Carbohydrates 8 g
   Fiber .5 g
   Fat 4 g
   Sodium 60 mg

Coconut Whipped Cream

Absolutely the best vegan whipped cream yet! Be sure to make this at least several hours ahead of time, then fluff with a whisk to produce a light and creamy whipped cream.

Ingredients

13.5-ounce can coconut milk
½ of 12.3-ounce package silken tofu, extra-firm
2½ tablespoons turbinado sugar
1 teaspoon vanilla extract
3 dashes salt
2 teaspoons Instant Clear Jel

Per 2 tablespoons:
    Calories 80
    Protein 1.5 g
    Carbohydrates 4 g
    Fiber 0 g
    Fat 7 g
    Sodium 55 mg

Steps

1 Blend first four ingredients until smooth in blender, then while still blending, sprinkle in Instant Clear Jel.

2 Chill to thicken. Stir briefly before serving.

Makes 12 servings.

Carob Fudge Sauce

Roma is an instant grain beverage that tastes much like coffee. Adding it to this recipe makes the fudge sauce taste much like its look-alike, the much-loved chocolate sauce. You'll be amazed.

Ingredients

3 tablespoons carob powder
¾ cup water
½ cup dates
1 tablespoon peanut or almond butter
1 teaspoon vanilla extract
⅛ teaspoon salt
1 teaspoon powdered coffee substitute (Roma)

Per 2 tablespoons:
Calories 40
Protein .5 g
Carbohydrates 9 g
Fiber 1 g
Fat 1 g
Sodium 35 mg

Variation: For *Carob Mint Sauce,* add ⅛ teaspoon peppermint extract. For *Carob Fudge Frosting,* decrease water to ½ cup.

Steps

1 Heat carob powder, water, and dates until dates are soft and carob mixture is glossy.

2 Combine this mixture with remaining ingredients in the blender and blend until smooth.

3 Store in refrigerator. Freezes well.

Makes 1½ cups.

Hot Fudge Sauce

Serve warm over non-dairy ice cream, cake, carob brownies, or thick smoothies. Much lower in fat and sugar than chocolate hot fudge sauce. Who's looking back now?

Ingredients

½ cup non-dairy carob chips
½ cup pitted dates
½ cup soymilk
¼ cup maple syrup
1 tablespoon almond butter
1 teaspoon vanilla extract
¹⁄₁₆ teaspoon salt

Per 2 tablespoons:
    Calories 110
    Protein 2 g
    Carbohydrates 17 g
    Fiber 1.5 g
    Fat 1.5 g
    Sodium 40 mg

Steps

1 Combine all ingredients in small saucepan.

2 Heat over medium heat until carob chips start to melt and dates become soft.

3 Pour mixture into blender and blend until smooth.

4 Sauce will thicken as it cools. Thin with soymilk when serving again.

Makes 1 ¼ cups.

Lemon Glaze

The perfect topping for the Frozen Lemon Custard, *page 215. Simple and delicious.*

Ingredients

½ cup pineapple juice
½ cup water
3 tablespoons lemon juice
3 tablespoons turbinado sugar
1 tablespoon cornstarch

Per 2 tablespoons:
  Calories 25
  Protein .1 g
  Carbohydrates 6.5 g
  Fiber 0 g
  Fat 0 g
  Sodium 2 mg

Steps

1 Bring the pineapple juice and water to a boil in a small saucepan. Add sugar and stir with a whisk to dissolve.

2 Mix lemon juice and cornstarch in a small bowl. Add to boiling liquid and stir until thickened.

3 Cool slightly before serving.

Makes 1 ¼ cups.

Puddings & Pies

Pecan Pie recipe on page 210

Butterscotch Pudding

The combination of maple and vanilla extract, plus just the right amount of salt, makes this pudding a dead ringer for butterscotch. Here's an opportunity to use maltitol to decrease the grams of sugar in the recipe. If you prefer, just use honey. Top this with Coconut Whipped Cream, *page 192, or make a parfait for a spectacular presentation.*

Ingredients

15-ounce can of pumpkin
3 tablespoons imitation honey
  (maltitol)
2 tablespoons honey
⅓ cup soymilk
1 teaspoon vanilla extract
½ teaspoon maple extract
⅛ teaspoon salt plus a dash

Per ½ cup:
  Calories 120
  Protein 2 g
  Carbohydrates 31 g
  Fiber 3.5 g
  Fat .5 g
  Sodium 370 mg

"Hast thou found honey? eat so much as is sufficient for thee."

—Proverbs 25:16

Steps

1 Whip all ingredients together in a bowl with a wire whisk.

2 For creamier pudding, add ⅓ cup silken tofu, 1 tablespoon more honey, and an additional dash of salt, then blend until smooth in blender.

Makes 4 servings.

Carob Pudding

Few desserts are as delicious and healthy as this one. Garnish with a few nuts or granola on top for a little crunch or layer in a parfait glass with whipped topping for a beautiful presentation.

Ingredients

¾ cup hot water
½ cup dates
2 tablespoons carob powder
1 tablespoon peanut butter
2 teaspoons powdered coffee
    substitute (Roma)
⅛ teaspoon salt
½ teaspoon vanilla
1 cup hot cooked millet
1 tablespoon coconut

Per serving:
    Calories 185
    Protein 3.5 g
    Carbohydrates 35 g
    Fiber 3 g
    Fat 4.5 g
    Sodium 100 mg

Steps

1 Soften dates by heating them together with the water.

2 Add remaining ingredients and blend smooth.

3 Serve warm or chilled.

Makes 4 servings.

Carob Delight

Three simple recipes are combined here to make a very special dessert. Butterscotch Pudding, page 197, can be substituted for the Carob Pudding for Butterscotch Delight!

Ingredients

1 recipe of *Grapenuts Crust I,* page 204
1 recipe of *Carob Pudding,* page 198
1 recipe of *Tofu Whipped Topping,* page 191
¾ cup toasted pecans, coarsely chopped

Per serving:
    Calories 180
    Protein 5 g
    Carbohydrates 16 g
    Fiber 3 g
    Fat 9 g
    Sodium 320 mg

Steps

1 Spoon in *Carob Pudding* into Grapenuts Crust and spread to edges.

2 Spread a layer of *Tofu Whipped Topping* on top, perhaps not the entire recipe, but according to your preference. Chill.

3 Just before serving, sprinkle toasted pecans on top.

Makes 16 servings.

COOK'S TIP

Coconut Whipped Cream, page 192, would also be an excellent choice for the topping.

Carob Mocha Mousse

Smooth and creamy goodness.

Ingredients

13.5-ounce can coconut milk
12.3 ounces firm, silken tofu
2 tablespoons honey
¼ cup soft pitted dates
½ teaspoon vanilla extract
1 tablespoon carob powder
1½ teaspoon powdered coffee
    substitute (Roma)
2 dashes of salt
2 teaspoons Instant Clear Jel

Per ½ cup:
    Calories 165
    Protein 5.5 g
    Carbohydrates 12 g
    Fiber 1 g
    Fat 12 g
    Sodium 65 mg

Steps

1 Whiz all ingredients, except Instant Clear Jel, in a blender until smooth.

2 Sprinkle in Instant Clear Jel while blender is running.

3 Pour into individual serving dishes, chill, and serve.

Makes 8 servings.

"Through the right exercise of the will, an entire change may be made in the lifestyle."

—John Scharffenberg, M.D.

Zinia's Rice Pudding

This authentic Spanish-style rice pudding involves a few steps, but it achieves a delicate texture and subtle vanilla flavor. View the StepFast Lifestyle Series, *program 11 video, for step-by-step Spanish cuisine instructions.*

Ingredients

1 cup short grain brown rice
3 cups soy or nut milk
1 cup coconut milk
½ teaspoon salt
⅓ cup turbinado sugar
1 teaspoon maple syrup
⅓ cup raisins
1 ½ teaspoons vanilla

Per ½ cup:
    Calories 190
    Protein 5 g
    Carbohydrates 29 g
    Fiber 2 g
    Fat 7 g
    Sodium 130 mg

Steps

1 Wash and soak the short grain brown rice in hot water for about ½ hour while you assemble the other ingredients.

2 Drain rice and put it in a mini-food processor and cut it to resemble couscous or millet.

3 Cook the rice with the 3 cups of milk, the coconut milk, and salt for 20 minutes on medium heat. Creamy pudding needs slow, gentle cooking so the rice is tender and the milk is reduced.

4 After the rice is cooked, remove from heat and add the remaining ingredients. The pudding might be a little soupy, but it will thicken as it cools.

Makes 10 servings.

Quick Rice Pudding

This version you can make in a jiffy!

Ingredients

13.5-ounce can coconut milk
1 cup vanilla Silk soymilk
1 tablespoon cornstarch
2 teaspoon vanilla extract
2 tablespoons maple syrup
⅛ teaspoon salt
¼ cup turbinado sugar
3 cups cooked brown rice
⅓ cup raisins (optional)

Per ½ cup:
- Calories 155
- Protein 3 g
- Carbohydrates 17 g
- Fiber 1 g
- Fat 9 g
- Sodium 145 mg

Steps

1 In a saucepan, heat all ingredients, except rice, over medium heat, stirring constantly until thickened.

2 Add cooked brown rice and continue stirring to heat thoroughly.

3 Add raisins if desired. Chill before serving.

Makes 10 servings.

HEALTH TIP

Find a convenient time and place to exercise. Try to make it a habit, but be flexible. If you miss an exercise opportunity, work activity into your day another way, like gardening or raking.

Flaky Pie Crust

The lemon juice adds no tartness but contributes to a flaky texture.

Ingredients

1⅛ cups whole wheat pastry flour
⅓ cup unbleached flour
¼ teaspoon salt
¼ cup light olive oil
¼ cup water
1 teaspoon lemon juice

Per ⅛ recipe:
    Calories 130
    Protein 9 g
    Carbohydrates 16 g
    Fiber 2 g
    Fat 6 g
    Sodium 75 mg

Steps

1 Mix the flours and the salt in a medium bowl. Add remaining ingredients at the same time and stir until well mixed.

2 With your hands, press into a small ball. Place ball between two sheets of waxed paper. Dampen the tabletop to prevent the dough from slipping and roll it out.

3 Roll the ball out into a 10-inch circle. Remove the top sheet of waxed paper and place the crust in a 9-inch pie plate.

4 Bake at 350° for 20 minutes for a baked pie shell or fill with filling and bake according to recipe.

Makes 1 pie crust.

"Listen carefully to Me, and eat what is good, and let your soul delight itself in abundance."

—*Isaiah 55:2*

Grapenuts Pie Crust I

This version closely resembles a graham cracker crust, but it offers whole grain goodness. For a finer texture, use 2½ cups of whole grain flake cereal.

Ingredients

1½ cups Grapenuts cereal
2 pitted dates
2–3 tablespoons water
⅓ cup English walnuts
¼ teaspoon salt

Per ¹⁄₁₀ pie crust:
    Calories 90
    Protein 3 g
    Carbohydrates 3 g
    Fiber 2 g
    Fat 3 g
    Sodium 150 mg

Steps

1 Preheat oven to 350°.

2 Place dates and water in a cereal bowl and microwave 1 minute to soften.

3 Grind walnuts and Grapenuts in food processor until fine.

4 Add dates and water and process until they will stick together when pressed.

5 Press into oil-sprayed pie plate or spring-form pan lined with parchment paper.

6 Bake for 15 minutes. It burns easily, so watch carefully.

Makes 1 crust.

Grapenuts Pie Crust II

This crust is plain and simple but quite tasty, with a nice texture too.

Ingredients

1½ cups Grapenuts cereal
⅓ cup pineapple or apple juice
1 tablespoon honey

Per ⅛ piecrust:
    Calories 90
    Protein 3 g
    Carbohydrates 5.5 g
    Fiber 2.5 g
    Fat .5 g
    Sodium 115 mg

Steps

1 Combine cereal, juice, and honey in mixing bowl and stir to mix well.

2 Press into pie plate with the back of a large spoon. Pour in filling and chill.

Makes 1 crust.

Crumble Nut Crust

Gluten-free goodness!

Ingredients

½ cup unsweetened coconut
½ cup raw almonds
½ cup brown rice flour
½ teaspoon salt (scant)
2 tablespoons honey
2 tablespoons water

Per ⅛ pie crust:
    Calories 210
    Protein 4 g
    Carbohydrates 19.5 g
    Fiber 3.9 g
    Fat 4 g
    Sodium 110 mg

Steps

1 Place coconut, almonds, flour, and salt in food processor. Blend together for about 30 seconds.

2 Add honey and process about 15 seconds more. Add water and blend again.

3 Press into a lightly oiled, 9-inch pie plate, shaping with fingers to make a nicely formed pie crust.

4 Bake at 375° for 10 minutes.

Makes 1 pie crust.

Blackberry Cobbler

My mother was known for her Southern charm and hospitality, and she loved the arrival of summer when she could make a blackberry "roll." What she meant was blackberry cobbler. By any name, it's a yummy summertime favorite that can be served year round since frozen blackberries are always available. But half the fun is picking the blackberries, which are organic and free, so if possible, mid-summer, head for the berry patch!

Ingredients

Crust:
2¼ cups whole wheat pastry flour
¾ cup unbleached flour
¾ teaspoon salt
½ cup light olive oil
½ cup plus 1 tablespoon cold water
2 teaspoons lemon juice

Filling:
7 cups blackberries, fresh or frozen
⅓ cup white grape raspberry juice
    concentrate
2 tablespoons instant tapioca
½ teaspoons stevia powder
1 tablespoon light olive oil
2 dashes of salt

Per ¹⁄₁₀ pie crust:
    Calories 90
    Protein 3 g
    Carbohydrates 3 g
    Fiber 2 g
    Fat 3 g
    Sodium 440 mg

COOK'S TIP

3 tablespoons turbinado sugar
can be substituted for the stevia.

Steps

1 Mix the flours and the salt in a medium bowl. Add the remaining ingredients and stir until well mixed. With your hands, press in a smooth ball.

2 Divide the ball of dough in two and form two balls. Place one ball of dough between two sheets of waxed paper. Dampen the tabletop to prevent the dough from slipping as you roll it out.

3 Roll the first ball into a 10-inch circle. Remove the top sheet of waxed paper. Place the crust in an oil-sprayed 9-inch deep dish pie plate.

4 Fill with the blackberries, which have been mixed well with the other filling ingredients.

5 Roll out the top crust and place over the filling. Trim with scissors leaving ½ inch beyond the pie plate. Pinch the top and bottom crusts together along the edge. Cut 5 vents in the top crust with a sharp knife and decorate with leaves cut from the extra dough.

6 Bake at 350° for 1 hour. Serve warm with *Vanilla Ice Cream,* page 218.

Makes 10 servings.

Frozen Carob Mousse Pie

The texture is firm, but creamy and the flavor is wonderfully rich. Keep one of these in the freezer for unexpected guests.

Ingredients

1½ packages of 12.3 ounces firm, silken tofu
¼ cup soymilk
¾ cup carob chips
1 cup pitted dates
⅓ cup almond butter
½ teaspoon salt (scant)
1½ teaspoons vanilla extract
1½ teaspoons powdered coffee substitute (Roma)
1 baked pie shell

Per slice:
    Calories 330
    Protein 10 g
    Carbohydrates 26 g
    Fiber 5 g
    Fat 15 g
    Sodium 600 mg

Steps

1 In a saucepan, heat first 4 ingredients until chips are melted.

2 Blend in blender with remaining ingredients until smooth and pour into baked pie shell.

3 Freeze until firm. Serve with *Coconut Whipped Cream*, page 192, and toasted pecans.

Makes 10 servings.

HEALTH TIP

Tofu is rich in high-quality protein and is a good source of B vitamins and iron. One-fourth pound of tofu contains 40 mg of healthy isoflavones, has almost no saturated fat and, of course, has no cholesterol.

Lemon Custard Pie

Rich and creamy, for very special occasions with a light meal.

Ingredients

20-ounce can sliced pineapple, drained
½ tablespoon fresh lemon rind
13.5-ounce can coconut milk
¼ teaspoon salt, slightly heaping
⅓ cup honey
4½ tablespoons cornstarch
4 tablespoons fresh lemon juice
1/16 teaspoon turmeric
1 pie crust

Per slice, with *Grapenuts Piecrust I,* page 204:
  Calories 300
  Protein 4 g
  Carbohydrates 32 g
  Fiber 3.5 g
  Fat 14 g
  Sodium 200 mg

Steps

1 In blender, blend all filling ingredients until smooth.

2 Cook mixture in a saucepan over medium heat until thick. Pour into a baked pie shell and chill until set.

Makes 8 servings.

Lemon Pineapple Pie

The first vegetarian cookbook I ever used was Joann Rachor's Of These Ye May Freely Eat. *It's full of many great recipes, including this one.*

Ingredients

2½ cups pineapple juice
½ cup rinsed, raw cashews
3 tablespoons lemon juice
2 tablespoons honey
1 teaspoon vanilla
½ cup water
¼ teaspoon salt
⅓ cup cornstarch
¼ teaspoon lemon extract
    or 1 teaspoon lemon rind
¾ cup crushed pineapple, in juice

Per ⅛ pie:
    Calories 175
    Protein 3 g
    Carbohydrates 28 g
    Fiber 1 g
    Fat 6.5 g
    Sodium 75 mg

Steps

1 Pour 2 cups of the pineapple juice into a saucepan. Bring to a boil.

2 While juice is heating, combine all remaining ingredients, except the crushed pineapple, in the blender and blend smooth.

3 Add the blended mixture to the boiling juice and then cook and stir until thickened. Stir in well-drained pineapple.

4 Pour into prepared pie shell and chill or serve in custard dishes.

Makes 8 servings.

COOK'S TIP

Serve with *Tofu Whipped Topping,* page 191. Pie can also be garnished with coconut, mandarin oranges and/or kiwi. If served as a pudding, top with Grapenuts or granola.

Pecan Pie

Pecan pie was my mother's calling card. Every new family in the neighborhood, the parents of every new baby, and those gathering for our family reunions had the privilege of enjoying some of her pecan pie. And I am happy to inform you, that Mama put her stamp of approval, a bright and beautiful smile on her face, on this vegan version.

Ingredients

1½ cups water
6 tablespoons flaxseed
1⅓ cups maple syrup
1½ cups pitted dates
1 teaspoon vanilla extract
1 teaspoon maple extract
1 teaspoon salt
½ cup water (additional)
5 tablespoons cornstarch
2 cups pecans, coarsely broken
3 tablespoons maple syrup
    (additional)
1 *Flaky Pie Crust,* page 203

Per ⅛ pie:
    Calories 175
    Protein 3 g
    Carbohydrates 28 g
    Fiber 1 g
    Fat 7 g
    Sodium 75 mg

COOK'S TIP

This pie has healthful ingredients, but it is also very rich. Serve small servings on a special occasion with a menu that is low in fat.

Steps

1 Combine water and flaxseed in saucepan. Bring to a boil and continue boiling and stirring until thick, about 5 minutes. Pour into blender and blend until smooth.

2 Add the maple syrup, dates, extracts, salt, additional ½ cup of water, and the cornstarch to the flaxseed mixture and blend until smooth.

3 Toast pecans in a 300° oven for 10 minutes.

4 Place pecans into a separate bowl and pour maple syrup and a sprinkle of salt over them. Stir to coat well. Reserve to place on top of filling.

5 Preheat oven to 350°. Partially bake a 9-inch pie shell, about 8 minutes.

6 Pour filling into the pie shell. Bake for 15 minutes.

7 Remove from oven and gently arrange coated pecans on top of filling, pressing slightly into filling.

8 Bake for 20 more minutes or until set. Cool before serving. Serve at room temperature with *Coconut Whipped Cream,* page 192.

Makes 12 servings.

Pecan Pie pictured on page 196

Frozen Treats

Frozen Lemon Custard recipe on page 215

Strawberry Smoothie

This classic smoothie can be made with frozen fruits of your choice. The bananas give it the smooth, creamy texture, and the berries or tropical fruits, like mango or kiwi, will give it color and distinctive flavor.

Ingredients

1 cup pineapple juice
2 frozen bananas
8 large frozen strawberries, slightly
  thawed

Per serving:
    Calories 90
    Protein 1 g
    Carbohydrates 23 g
    Fiber 2 g
    Fat .2 g
    Sodium 2 mg

"A cheerful heart is good medicine..."

    —Proverbs 17:22 (NIV)

COOK'S TIP

To freeze bananas, peel ripe bananas, place into a plastic bag, and freeze. I like to slice them before freezing them so I can skip that step when making frozen treats.

Steps

1 Slice frozen bananas into ½-inch slices and place them in a blender.

2 Add pineapple juice and strawberries, then blend all ingredients into a thick shake.

3 Garnish each serving with granola, if desired.

Makes 4 servings.

Orange Crush

A happy ending to a hot, sunny day.

Ingredients

½ cup orange juice concentrate
½ frozen banana
2 cups soymilk
1 teaspoon vanilla extract
A dash of salt
12 ice cubes

Per serving:
    Calories 265
    Protein 11 g
    Carbohydrates 45.5 g
    Fiber 4.5 g
    Fat 5 g
    Sodium 110 mg

Steps

1 Cut the banana into chunks.

2 In a blender, blend smooth all ingredients except the ice.

3 Gradually add ice as you blend, until thick.

4 Garnish with fresh orange slices.

Makes 2 servings.

Piña Colada

Asian paper umbrellas make this a fun supper drink that you can eat with a spoon.

Ingredients

1 cup pineapple juice
½ cup coconut milk
2 frozen bananas
¼ teaspoon coconut extract

Per serving:
  Calories 250
  Protein 3 g
  Carbohydrates 46 g
  Fiber 3.5 g
  Fat 9 g
  Sodium 3 mg

Steps

1 Slice bananas into chunks, combine with remaining ingredients in a blender, and blend smooth.

2 Add more or fewer banana chunks according to desired consistency.

3 For firmer consistency, place thick mixture directly into freezer and freeze for 30 to 60 minutes.

Makes 2 servings.

HEALTH TIP

Adults should consume about 4,500 milligrams of potassium each day. We all know that bananas are an excellent source of potassium. A medium banana contains 450 mg, but a medium baked potato provides 800 mg.

Frozen Lemon Custard

These individual desserts can be made ahead to give the royal treatment to even unexpected guests, who will never guess they are eating tofu!

Ingredients

12.3 ounces firm, silken tofu
¼ cup lemon juice
3 tablespoons honey
3 tablespoons light olive oil
1/16 teaspoon salt
1 teaspoon fresh lemon rind
A dash of turmeric
⅓ cup chopped nuts

Per serving:
    Calories 165
    Protein 8 g
    Carbohydrates 9 g
    Fiber 1.5 g
    Fat 12 g
    Sodium 25 mg

Steps

1 Place all ingredients, except nuts, in a blender and blend until smooth.

2 Line muffin tin with 8 paper muffin cups. Sprinkle chopped nuts into the bottom of each muffin cup and pour tofu mixture into the cups.

3 Place in freezer for several hours or until set.

4 Serve with *Lemon Glaze*, page 195, *Carob Fudge Sauce*, page 193, or *Berry Fruit Sauce*, page 189.

Makes 8 servings.

Pineapple Sorbet

This all-fruit frozen treat is a perfect light dessert.

Ingredients

20-ounce can crushed pineapple,
   in juice

Per ½ cup:
   Calories 85
   Protein .5 g
   Carbohydrates 22 g
   Fiber 1 g
   Fat .1 g
   Sodium 1 mg

Steps

1 Spoon crushed pineapple with the juice into an ice tray. Freeze solid.

2 Run frozen pineapple cubes through a Champion juicer, or allow to thaw slightly, and purée in a blender.

3 Serve with granola or whole grain crackers.

Makes 4 servings.

HEALTH TIP

Between meals, be sure to drink plenty of water, about 1 ounce for every 2 pounds of body weight daily. With meals, drink no more than ½ cup of liquid for optimum digestion.

Strawberry Sorbet

This recipe has been shared by the Lifestyle Center of America, and it is delightfully smooth and creamy.

Ingredients

6 small frozen bananas, sliced
    (3 cups)
1½ cups frozen strawberries
½ cup dairy-free milk powder
Pinch of salt
¼ cup white grape raspberry frozen
    juice concentrate

Per ½ cup:
    Calories 70
    Protein 2 g
    Carbohydrates 15.5 g
    Fiber 2 g
    Fat 1 g
    Sodium 10 mg

Steps

1 Slightly thaw the bananas and strawberries.

2 Blend all the ingredients in a food processor or blender.

3 Pour into a container and freeze.

4 Slightly thaw and serve with an ice cream scoop.

Makes 10 servings.

Variation: Substitute peaches for strawberries and add ½ teaspoon of almond extract for *Peach Sorbet.*

Vanilla Ice Cream

Delicious with fresh peaches or Hot Fudge Sauce, *page 194!*

Ingredients

1 cup raw almonds
1 can coconut milk
⅓ cup honey
2 teaspoons vanilla
½ teaspoon stevia powder
¼ teaspoon salt

Per ½-cup serving:
    Calories 160
    Protein 3.5 g
    Carbohydrates 11 g
    Fiber 1 g
    Fat 12 g
    Sodium 55 mg

Steps

1 Blend all ingredients in blender until smooth.

2 Gradually add 5 cups of ice cubes, blending until smooth and thick.

3 Serve immediately for "soft serve" texture. Pour into container and freeze 2 to 3 hours for firmer consistency. If completely frozen, allow to thaw at room temperature for about 30 minutes.

Makes 6 cups.

HEALTH TIP

Heart disease is no longer just for men. It is indeed the leading cause of death among American women. Fortunately, there are lifestyle measures that will help to prevent heart disease, including a total vegetarian diet!

Old-fashioned Ice Cream

With this old-fashioned ice cream, you can make any flavor. If you have a hand-crank ice cream freezer, that's all the better. Everyone can get some exercise while the excitement mounts!

Ingredients

3 13.5-ounce cans coconut milk
3 cans full of vanilla Silk soymilk
¾ cup turbinado sugar
1 tablespoon vanilla extract
¼ teaspoon salt
2 tablespoons light olive oil

Per ½ cup:
    Calories 170
    Protein 39 g
    Carbohydrates 12 g
    Fiber .5 g
    Fat 13 g
    Sodium 4 mg

Variation: To make *Peach Ice Cream,* freeze the custard, then add 1 cup diced fresh peaches and 1 teaspoon almond extract, mix well, and place ice cream in the freezer.

Steps

1 Blend all ingredients in blender to dissolve sugar.

2 Pour into an ice cream freezer. Freeze as with conventional ice cream recipe, using ice and rock salt, for about 45 minutes.

Makes 22 servings.

COOK'S TIP

An alternate method of freezing is to pour into ice trays and freeze. Then run the cubes though a Champion juicer, or thaw slightly and purée in a blender with a small amount of soymilk.

Banana Split

Who would have thought a healthy diet could include a banana split! But as you can see, this version is mostly fruit and nuts and is chock-full of vitamins, minerals, and antioxidants. A "cool" gathering is to have a banana split party and let everyone make their own.

Ingredients

1 banana
1 cup *Strawberry Sorbet,* page 217, or non-dairy frozen dessert of your choice
1 tablespoon *Carob Fudge Sauce,* page 193
1 tablespoon crushed pineapple, drained
1 tablespoon *Strawberry Jam,* page 190
1 tablespoon granola or chopped nuts

Per banana split:
   Calories 340
   Protein 5 g
   Carbohydrates 73 g
   Fiber 6 g
   Fat 7 g
   Sodium 70 mg

Steps

1 Slice banana lengthwise and place in banana split dish.

2 Top with 3 small scoops of sorbet, then spoon on toppings.

Makes 1 banana split.

COOK'S TIP

If banana split dishes are not available, most ice cream stores will sell plastic banana boats for a modest cost.

Planning Your Menu

One of the keys to implementing a total vegetarian diet is to plan ahead. Be sure to have the necessary ingredients on hand and consider preparing a large amount of a basic ingredient with several recipes in mind.

Here are some suggestions for multiple recipes:

- Cook a large crockpot of pinto beans to use in soups, salads, and burritos.

- A large pot of cooked millet could be used first for breakfast cereal, then for *Millet Loaf*, and finally, for *Carob Pudding*. The proportion for cooking millet is 1 cup of millet to 3 cups of water; cook over medium-low heat for 30 minutes.

- *Baked Brown Rice* can be used in a number of dishes as well, such as *Holiday Loaf*, *Quick Rice Pudding*, and the quick version of *Spanish Rice*.

HEARTY BREAKFASTS

- *Baked Oatmeal* (pg. 50)
- *Fruit Salad* (pg. 84)
- *Granola* (pg. 51–53)
- Ground Flax Seed
- *Soymilk* (pg. 33)

- *Crockpot Cereal* (pg. 48)
- Ground Flax Seed
- *Granola* (pg. 51–53)
- Whole Grain Bagel
- Almond Butter
- Fresh Fruit

- *Stoplight Tofu* (pg. 39)
- *Oven Roasted Potatoes* (pg. 156)
- Sliced Tomatoes
- Whole Wheat Toast
- *Strawberry Jam* (pg. 190)

- *Belgian Waffles* (pg. 44)
- *Berry Fruit Sauce* (pg. 189)
- Fresh Fruit
- Almond Butter
- *Best Oat Sausage* (pg. 129)
  (See variation for Best Oat Burgers, pg. 129)

- *Linguine with Artichoke Hearts* (pg. 117)
- Tossed Salad
- *Italian Dressing* (pg. 89)
- Steamed Asparagus
- *Vegan Tiramisu* (pg. 186)

COME FOR DINNER!

- *Sweet & Sour Soy Curls* (pg. 135)
- *Baked Brown Rice* (pg. 159)
- *Spinach Salad* (pg. 85)
- *Carob Pudding* (pg. 198)
- *Granola Topping* (pg. 51–53)

- *Broccoli Soup* (pg. 105)
- *Pita Chips* (pg. 65)
- *Stuffed Mushrooms* (pg. 123)
- *Beets & Baby Greens Salad* (pg. 86)
- *Butterscotch Pudding* (pg. 197)

- *Best Oat or Garden Burgers* (pg. 129–130)
- Corn on the Cob
- *Tofu Mayonnaise* (pg. 74)
- *Veggie Platter with Onion Dill Dip* (pg. 75)
- *Happy Cookies* (pg. 180)

LET'S HAVE A PICNIC!

Happy Thanksgiving!

- *Baked Tofu* (pg. 131)
- *Holiday Loaf* (pg. 125)
- *Herb Gravy* (pg. 169)
- *Sweet Potato Soufflé* (pg. 167)
- Steamed Broccoli
- *Beets & Baby Greens Salad* (pg. 86)
- *Ruby Raspberry Dressing* (pg. 87)
- *Pecan Pie* (pg. 210)
- *Coconut Whipped Cream* (pg. 192)

Company's Coming!

- *Millet Loaf* (pg. 126)
- *Herb Gravy* (pg. 169)
- Steamed Zucchini & Onions
- *Fresh Cranberry Relish* (pg. 168)
- Whole Wheat Rolls
- *Tofu Cheesecake* (pg. 185)
- *Berry Fruit Sauce* (pg. 189)

Relax with Haystacks!

- *Crockpot Beans* (pg. 136)
- Baked Tostitos Corn Chips
- Shredded Lettuce
- Diced Tomatoes
- Chopped Onions
- Sliced Black Olives
- *Healthy Melty Cheese* (pg. 171)
- *Salsa* (pg. 80)

Cool Down with Summer Fare!

- *Tofu Egg Salad Sandwiches* (pg. 95)
- *Tomato Basil Salad* (pg. 96)
- Celery Stuffed with Almond Butter
- *Baked Lay's Chips*
- *Carob Brownies* (pg. 181)

- *Soy Curls Salad* (pg. 94)
- Fruit Kabobs
- Sliced Tomatoes
- Whole Wheat Bread
- Black Olives
- *Vanilla Ice Cream* (pg. 218)

Bridal Brunch

- *Minced Tofu Spread* (pg. 76)
- *Tofu Egg Salad Tea Sandwiches* (pg. 95)
- *Fruit Platter with Creamy Lemon Dip* (pg. 69)
- Fresh Roasted Nuts
- *Black Forest Cake* (pg. 184)
- *Raspberry Zinger Punch* (pg. 30)

Kids' Stuff

- *Jungle Gems* (pg. 142)
- *Zucchini Patties* (pg. 148)
- *Honey Wheat Bread* (pg. 55)
- *Beans 'n Franks* (pg. 147)
- *Caramel Corn* (pg. 150)

- *Alphabet Soup* (pg. 145)
- *Hummus and Veggies* (pg. 71)
- *Dirt Pudding* (pg. 153)

Index

RESOURCES for a Happier, Healthier, and Fuller LIFE

StepFast Lifestyle Series DVD
This dynamic, interactive 12-part health-revitalizing series teaches you how to live in harmony with the natural laws of health! Learn to enjoy a delicious, plant-based diet; engage in a simple, energizing exercise program; and be empowered by a disciplined spiritual life. You will also receive tips on natural remedies and herbs, with presentations on heart disease, weight control, diabetes, hypertension, cancer, osteoporosis, and more. Includes *StepFast Seminar Guide,* with step-by-step instructions on how to conduct a StepFast Lifestyle Seminar and the *StepFast Resource Guide on CD-ROM,* which includes recipes, fitness materials, and more.

DV-SFP $89.99

Total Vegetarian Cookbook, StepFast Lifestyle Series DVD, and Apron
Buy all three together and save $25!

MS-TVSF......... $109.99

StepFast 3 Pocket Apron
MS-SFA.... $19.99

To Order:
www.AmazingFacts.org
800-538-7275

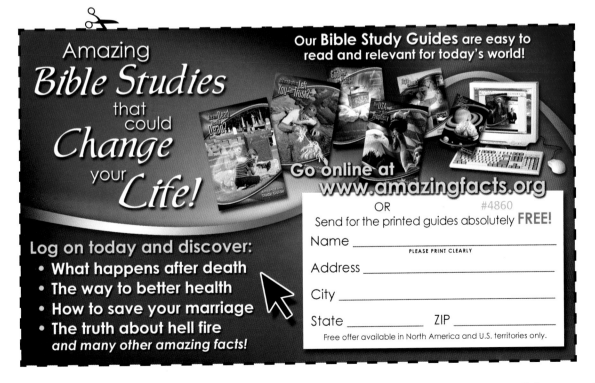

Amazing **Bible Studies** that could *Change* your *Life!*

Our **Bible Study Guides** are easy to read and relevant for today's world!

Go online at **www.amazingfacts.org**

OR   #4860
Send for the printed guides absolutely **FREE!**

Name _____
PLEASE PRINT CLEARLY
Address _____
City _____
State _____ ZIP _____
Free offer available in North America and U.S. territories only.

Log on today and discover:
- **What happens after death**
- **The way to better health**
- **How to save your marriage**
- **The truth about hell fire**
  and many other amazing facts!

P.O. Box 909
ROSEVILLE, CA 95678-0909

Notes

240　Notes